CONTENTS

MONSTER TERROR

PSYCHOLOGICAL THRILLER

ACKNOWLEDGMENTS

For encouragement and assistance in preparing this volume, the editors owe special thanks to the following persons: Ronald Gottesman, for his continuing interest in this project from the start and valuable suggestions for materials to be included; James D. Allen and Kay Hines, for translating material from French and German; Joseph Fisch and Kathy Collins, for ably assisting in research; Claudia Wilson, our editor at Prentice-Hall, for exercising wisdom and forbearance through the various stages of production; and Rhoda Ross, who virtually shared with one of the editors his part in shaping this book.

We wish also to thank the staff of the Theater-Film Research Division of the Library of the Performing Arts at Lincoln Center; the director of the Film Study Center at the Museum of Modern Art; and the Dean of Faculty at Queens College, for providing research aid.

Introduction
by T. J. ROSS

Among the longest-lived of film genres, the horror film continues to enjoy the best of health. In recent years it has in fact flourished at the box office at a time of increasing commercial risk for every kind of film-making venture. Further evidence of the genre's vitality is the critical interest in its history and art shown by a growing part of the film audience. And it is with such a sizeable audience in mind, whose taste for horror films remains undiminished but not unselective, that some of the most gifted of the younger filmmakers have been drawn to working within the conventions of the form.

Thus, the latest (1971) film adaptation of *Dr. Jekyll and Mr. Hyde* —entitled *I, Monster* and starring two veterans of British horror movies, Peter Cushing and Christopher Lee—was directed by twenty-two-year-old Stephen Weeks. Two recent entries in the Dracula sweepstakes, *Countess Dracula* and *Taste the Blood of Dracula,* were made by another director in his twenties presently working in England, Hungarian-born Peter Sasdy. And an earlier group of even more astonishing horror films was completed by Michael Reeves shortly before his death in his mid-twenties. His *Witchfinder General* and *The Sorcerers* mark a by now legendary achievement in the British terror-suspense cinema of the sixties.[1]

Perhaps the best known of the younger American directors who have worked with the genre is Peter Bogdanovich, whose first feature film, *Targets,* is discussed in this volume by Brian Henderson. Another filmmaker who has brought together his talents as critic and director in the making of horror films is Curtis Harrington. Chiefly known for his experimental short films, Harrington has

---

[1] Michael Reeves's films are discussed at length by Robin Wood in *Movie,* No. 17 (Winter, 1969–70): 2–6; for a fuller discussion of younger British directors concentrating on the horror film, see David Pirie, "New Blood," in *Sight and Sound,* Spring, 1971, pp. 73–75.

broken through to a broader audience with a horror film, *What's the Matter with Helen?* which proved to be one of the most powerful films of 1971 in any category. We are pleased to include some of his early impressions of horror movies in this collection.

Our first group of essays map out leading patterns of development in the history of horror films; the essays also offer theoretical perspectives on content and style. Throughout these pieces on "the horror domain," certain titles recur—titles of those films which have clearly proved of "more than passing interest" and which, in the enthusiastic response they invariably evoke from both critics and general audiences, stand as key works for any discussion of the genre. Many of the films thus briefly referred to are more fully treated in essays in later sections.

In our section on "Gothic Horror," Jack Kerouac writes on the style and appeal of F. W. Murnau's silent masterpiece on vampirism, *Nosferatu.* Ernest Jones, in the passage included from his classic study, *On the Nightmare,* explores the vampire myth from a psychoanalytic viewpoint; and Roy Huss in his essay considers the same myth in its transmutations from the Victorian novel to the modern stage and screen. Michel Perez is concerned with some of the more provocative treatments of the Jekyll and Hyde story. Stephen Farber's remarks on "New American Gothic" deal, in contrast, with an imposing cycle of films centered (as are *Targets* and *What's the Matter with Helen?*) on anonymous characters whose twisted fantasies and actions reflect the aridness and terror of our daily landscape. But the main focus in this section is, inevitably, on the two most familiar and celebrated figures in the horror domain, the vampire and the Frankenstein monster.

II

Related to a line which runs from the Gothic novel to the theater of Georg Buechner to the work of such modern painters as Edvard Munch or James Ensor or Balthus, films of Gothic horror are expressionist in their style and atmosphere and humanist in the drive of their meaning and concern. They are most akin to expressionist art in their overriding emphasis on distorted emotional capacities and quests, on energies wildly miscast. Thus, their ominously stark landscapes are peopled by wailing giants, brutal hunchbacks, compulsive scientists, raging mobs, fierce dark ladies, and swooning blond heroines. Nor does the fevered pitch of the scene—and its shocks of horror—depend simply on the appearance or antics of a freakish-looking creature, but rather on a situation which determines the whole action of the film. We are more moved and scared by the freakishly profound isolation in which every one of the main characters is caught up than by a gimmickry of things that go bump in the night. Of course we rightly expect a horror film to contain the raw stuff of fright and suspense, such as long shadows flung on a wall, eerie-looking lab rooms, and characters possessing the sort of features and offbeat mannerisms that would delight the heart of a Fellini. Yet in the best examples of the genre, it is precisely through such shock tactics that the charge of meaning is released: the moral is inseparable from the terror.

Thus, to read the novel by Mary Shelley that in 1818 introduced Dr. Frankenstein and his creature to the world is to be struck by the number and variety of scenes of hearth and home it dwells on. The novel's ambience of horror indeed builds upon the ruins of one domestic scene after another—as each is denied or lost, first to the monster, then to his creator. What most affects us in both the novel and the first set of films it inspired (directed by James Whale) is the monster's anguish; and although the film monster's anguish is limited to the most primitive emotional plane (in contrast to Mary Shelley's monster, whose suffering is powered by capacities which are—inseparably—intellectual as well as emotional), the anguish of the creature on screen is nearly as moving. Perhaps because of its primitive level of articulation, it is all the more frightening. As different as they are otherwise in plot incidentals, book and film agree on the ultimate point of outrage: the denial to a creature made in the image of man of either home or homemaking Eve.

But, then, this sense of displacement from a home base and from nature is fundamental to the modern sensibility. The monster belongs to our age of moral and ecological chaos; and he roams the wild with a grotesque impassivity and disorientation altogether familiar in the myths and files of contemporary alienation. In this he anticipates a crowded gallery of types that would include, among recent examples, the character "Ratzo" played by Dustin Hoffman in *Midnight Cowboy*, whose limp seems a step-by-stomp borrowing of the walk adopted by Boris Karloff for his most celebrated role, and (like the monster's) suggests hobbled passions.

Nor is it the creature alone who is left stranded, but also the obsessive tinkerer who put him together. Concerning the meaning of

Dr. Frankenstein's life and deeds Mary Shelley is explicit, sounding the message which will echo, if in somewhat flatter accents, through countless mad scientist movies:

> If the study to which you apply yourself has a tendency to weaken your affections and to destroy your taste for those simple pleasures in which no alloy can possibly mix, then that study is certainly unlawful, that is to say, not befitting the human mind. . . . If no man allowed any pursuit whatsoever to interfere with the tranquillity of his domestic affections, Greece had not been enslaved; Caesar would have spared his country; America would have been discovered more gradually and the empires of Mexico and Peru had not been destroyed.

III

There is a short story by Nathaniel Hawthorne—"Rappaccini's Daughter"—which, like Mary Shelley's novel, has proved to be both typical and prophetic in its mixture of Gothic-horror ingredients. Indeed, the figure whom Hawthorne places in opposition to the rapacious and vampirelike Dr. Rappaccini, a wily but good man of science named Professor Baglioni, anticipates in role and manner that most formidable yet congenial of the opponents of Dracula, the good Dr. Van Helsing. And it is Professor Baglioni who gives us the word which, while it harks back to Mary Shelley's, at the same time points ahead to what was to be the next phase in horror films after their initial focus on the monster: the placing of the *creator* of monsters at the center of dramatic interest. As the good doctor warns us about the bad one:

> . . . I know that look of his: it is the same that coldly illuminates his face as he bends over a bird, a mouse or a butterfly which in pursuance of some experiment he has killed by the perfume of a flower—a look as deep as Nature itself, but without Nature's warmth of love. Signor, I will stake my life upon it, you are the subject of one of Rappaccini's experiments.

Far more numerous than his few portrayals of the Frankenstein monster are the roles which Karloff himself played as mad scientist —roles prefigured by the sinister dedications of a Dr. Frankenstein or Rappaccini. The thirties and early forties saw an abundant cycle of low-budget features centered on the mad scientist (played most frequently by Karloff, Bela Lugosi, or Lionel Atwill). Although many of these films maintain their appeal in the plasticity of their visual effects and the bite of their dialogue, they have not so far been accorded much critical comment or appreciation. Such films as *Bride of the Monster, The Mad Doctor of Market Street,* and *The Man Who Could Not Die* invariably center around an outcast from the scientific community, a disaffected professional, staking his all on the one mighty scientific breakthrough that would redeem his reputation. Or his motive might be shown to have degenerated to the level of revenge-seeking. A typically low-budget yet richly textured film in this line is a Karloff-Lugosi vehicle of the thirties, *Invisible Ray,* whose protagonist invents a machine which can be used as a wondrous cure-all against disease and yet radiates a power of such enormity that it can chip the edge off a star. In his drive to redeem both his name and his mother's faith, the outsider-protagonist ends up as a sinister and doomed revenger. The exchanges between him and the president of a scientific congress typify a recurrent note in these films:

"We have never seen eye to eye."
"That's because I've always looked two-hundred years ahead of you!"

Too far ahead of his scene to abide easily within it, the mad scientist nonetheless remains as courtly and vivaciously old world in manner as a Humbert Humbert. And that precisely is his trouble. Alive both to the anguish and beauty of the past and to the problematic yet compelling prospects of the future, he too feels stranded in—and so ends up contributing to—the horrors of the present.

One of the most famous films on mad scientism is Georges Franju's *Les Yeux Sans Visage* (shown in America as *The Horror Chamber of Dr. Faustus*). Raymond Durgnat's discussion of this most unnerving and poignant of horror films offers pointers toward an evaluation of such lesser-known American works as those noted above—not the least of which remarks is the clarification Durgnat offers on the paradoxes inherent in an aesthetics of horror.

IV

The prevailing mode of horror in the fifties diverged sharply from the humanist focus on the individual in his fate and feelings that distinguished the line of Gothic horror. Instead of a heroic conflict between individuals—monster versus Faustian or Faustian at odds with a society whose order and orders were rarely presented on screen as unqualifiedly justified—we have the simpler setup of some mutation of the animal species, or evil arrival from another planet, opposed to a faceless team representative of the home front, whose "order" is assumed without question to be the paramount value. This type of "monster-terror" film is, for all the frenzy of its action, relatively cold in tone. No serious thought of sidetracking or somehow harboring the creature (whether displaced dinosaur or planetary emissary) is ever entertained (or when someone does entertain the thought, he is doomed not to survive past the first reel); rather, once the thing is spotted, the message is to get it before it gets us.

In their response to the apocalyptic prospect of slumbering beasts roused or mutated by atomic blast, an interesting contrast may be noted between American movies and their Japanese counterparts. In the Japanese variety, such as the numerous sequels to the highly popular *Godzilla,* we do see a friendship struck up between a boy and a giant flying monster. From one sequel to the next, we see the boy and his community become as attached to the monster as kids on American TV are to Lassie. On the one hand, then, the response to the beast of apocalypse includes the fantasy of its domestication; on the other, the response is to entertain in all seriousness the fantasy of a do-or-die adventure, the challenge of one more heady rumble. And what applies to mutated beasts in American films applies equally to any luckless teenager who may happen to be transformed, through some lab mixup or the nefarious dealings of a science teacher, into a werewolf or other kind of wild, freakish being. As John Denne notes in "Society and the Monster," the common response to the adolescent transformed in style and appearance is violence.

Like the mad scientist movie, such mad mutant or beast-at-large films belong more to the horror domain than to science fiction proper since their whole intent is to express a terror rooted in the deepest of personal motives or "drives" rather than to depict the marvels (or threats) of technological advance as such. The sociologist Jacques Ellul has observed that machines may come to possess more interest—more "personality"—than the men who tend them. This would also seem to be a premise of Stanley Kubrick's science fiction film *2001,* in which we see a machine sensitive to the degree that it has, precisely, a *nervous* breakdown—the only hint of emotional life we are given in the whole film! In a horror movie there is never any such danger of supersession of human nerves—or interest —by the machine. As Kingsley Amis has noted of monsters and related mutants:

> They may get switched on by somebody who calls himself a scientist, but it is always taken for granted that the science is not real. Frankenstein's bubbling retorts and arcing terminals are understood as nothing more than a colorful and enjoyable prelude to the main business of the evening, a monster waking up and very soon turning unfriendly.

In science fiction, Amis goes on to say, "the science, however perfunctory or absurd, is meant to be taken as real." [2] Of all monster-terror movies *King Kong* still rules as the greatest. A product of the rich efflorescence of genre films in the thirties, *King Kong* presents its title beast as a child of, rather than mutation from, Nature. The perennial and complex appeal of this film (and its highly individualized beast) is attested to in the remarks of the late distinguished critic William Troy, on seeing the film during its first run; in the essay by the poet X. J. Kennedy, written a generation later; and in the closely wrought analysis by a contemporary French critic, Claude Ollier.

There certainly are Gothic-horror ingredients in *King Kong* and in the zombie country described by Michel Perez in "The Puritan Despair"; yet when we set *I Walked with a Zombie* in the context of "monster terror," we reinforce its stress on a confrontation of teams —of two civilizations. As Perez observes, its terror derives from the clear fact that there are no monsters on the scene, none other than the fundamental psychic states of the characters, whose psychology is rendered neither in clinical nor novelistic formulations. Instead, it gains its effects by a rhythmic flow of visual images that derive from the iconographies of popular art. Although both this film and *King Kong* are expressionist in style, they deal more with group actions and fears than with individual heroics or anguish; the very ordinariness of their group members in turn reduces the humanist perspectives and scale of the Gothic main line. In this way both movies anticipate the representative monster terror films of the fifties.

---

[2] Kingsley Amis, "Dracula, Frankenstein, Sons and Co.," in *Whatever Became of Jane Austen?* (London: Jonathan Cape, Ltd. 1970), p. 129.

Another work of Gothic distortion and power which is nonetheless included in the "terror" category is the Tod Browning classic *Freaks*. For once, we see a team of "monsters" united against the threatening incursions among them of a single "human"! The latter is a circus beauty "icily regular" in feature, whose fatal mistake is to remain imperceptive about the humanity (and therefore danger) of the irregularly formed beings whom she seeks to betray. John Thomas's sensitive analysis of the film suggests the power of its nuanced and harrowing effects.

V

As with Gothic horror, the psychological thriller offers more than a game of Funhouse shocks. In a notable thriller of the fifties, *The Incredible Shrinking Man*, for example, we find a mordantly ironic play on the themes of identity and insecure sexuality. The film gives us a protagonist who grows in self-awareness as he shrivels in size. Thus, the more he dwindles, the more he gains through his "raised consciousness" an enterprising spirit and physical courage. No more than Hitchcock's *Psycho* nor Jacques Tourneur's *Leopard Man* does this film pretend to any sort of realistic documentation of a psychological case.

The psychological thriller defines itself indeed by the distance it keeps from clinical psychology. Psychological thrillers are so designated because they deal with (in the current jargon) obviously "disturbed" protagonists; the nature of their disturbance, however, is never explained in any realistic sense. This is as true of one of the first and greatest of such films, Fritz Lang's *M*, as it is of Polanski's *Repulsion* or Bogdanovich's *Targets* (a point each of the writers on these two films is at pains to stress).

The tacking on of an explanatory note, as at the end of *Psycho*, is likely to work against the grain of the film. Critics have often remarked on the vitiating effect of *Psycho*'s final scene, in which a psychologist feeds us a boringly official solution to a horror which had hitherto hit with the force of a mystery as inexorable and terrible in its "rightness" as the suspense of a classical tragedy. The essay in our opening section by R. H. W. Dillard reminds us of the degree to which we respond, in the most accomplished of horror films, to a poetry of "disturbance" that presses toward a metaphysical dimension. Or, just as compellingly, toward the deepest of social questions, such as those raised, as noted earlier, by the more terror-istic aspects of the everyday industrial landscape. It is through this kind of landscape that the protagonists of Polanski—or of Bogdano-vich or Curtis Harrington—are doomed to move and have their being.

The best horror films, then, seek neither to dissipate nor to ex-plain away in simplistic formulations the mystery of their night-mare worlds. But this is not to say that they trade in obscurity; rather, their effects can attain to an illuminating and purgative power. In a brilliant review of an early psychological thriller *Night Must Fall* (1937), the critic Otis Ferguson described the film as work-ing on the audience

> . . . almost with the surgeon's healing function . . . because those who would appear in headlines simply as fiends or fools reveal themselves gradually here in impulses common to all humanity, but warped into the unspeakable by simple inner and outward pressures as of some bedevilling bone against the brain or of some stored-up wrong, old envy, hatred, frustration. So they are to be understood and, even when most pitiless and terrible, pitied. . . .[3]

VI

One aspect of horror films—as of the film genres in general—that clearly invites further study is the difference in national approaches to the same set of conventions. We earlier noted, for example, a dif-ference between American and Japanese films in their treatment of monster-terror plots. Another difference between American and Brit-ish horror films may be seen in the two main directions in which the genre now seems to be moving. One, as exemplified by a film like *Targets,* is away from the glamor of Transylvanian never-never lands or apocalyptic sensationalism and toward a relatively low-keyed, realistic focus on the monstrousness of the commonplace.

The other trend—most evident so far in British films—is toward a more open and calculated play on sexual themes. In British films from *Horror of Dracula* (1958) to *Taste the Blood of Dracula*

[3] Otis Ferguson, "Montgomery in the Movies," in *The Film Criticism of Otis Ferguson,* edited by Robert Wilson (Philadelphia: Temple University Press, 1971), p. 178.

(1971), the title creature has been appearing more and more like a Don Juan with fangs. And just as the sardonic mood and wit expressed in "black humor" served as a background accompaniment to the insistent sexual candor of the sixties, so too the same kind of humor has accompanied the sexual overtones of recent horror fare. Edged with a post-Freudian sexual nihilism, this kind of humor is on a different wavelength from the humor found in early classics like *The Bride of Frankenstein*.

An increased social orientation and a greater emphasis on sexual *faisandage*—these are the present trends. Yet as a form hardly past the half-century mark in age, the horror film remains invitingly rich and open in its possibilities. What Roy Huss and I have chiefly aimed for in editing this book is to trace the vital lines of development of a form still in the process of evolving rather than to lay down hard and fast rules or final definitions. We have sought throughout approaches which might suggest further paths for exploration rather than closed classifications.

Certainly, in each of its modes and levels of ambition, from *Nosferatu* to *Invisible Ray* to *The Birds*, the horror film has brought to worldwide audiences the pleasures which inhere in aesthetic play and shocks of perception; and it is clearly a shared motive of the pieces which follow to add to our pleasure in the art of the genre.

Chronology

1818   Publication of Mary Shelley's *Frankenstein.*

1849   Death of Edgar Allan Poe.

1886   Publication of Robert Louis Stevenson's *The Strange Case of Dr. Jekyll and Mr. Hyde.*

1897   Publication of Bram Stoker's *Dracula.*

1908   *Dr. Jekyll and Mr. Hyde* (USA). Fifteen-minute film based on the 1887 play. First of ten film versions of the story.

1910   *Frankenstein* (USA). The Edison Company's famous "lost film" version of Mary Shelley's novel.

1912   *The Conquest of the Pole* (France). Georges Méliès's film employing a huge mechanical, man-devouring arctic monster.

1915   *Life Without Soul* (USA). Five-reel version of Mary Shelley's *Frankenstein.*

1919   *The Cabinet of Dr. Caligari* (Germany). Landmark expressionist film, with the monster as somnambulist.

1920   *The Golem* (Germany). Paul Wegener's remake of his own 1914 version. Exerted a strong influence on James Whale's *Frankenstein* (1931).

1922   *Nosferatu* (Germany). Murnau's expressionistic masterpiece based very loosely on Bram Stoker's *Dracula.*

1925   *The Phantom of the Opera* (USA). Lon Chaney's debut as a full-fledged horror film star.

1927   Broadway opening of stage adaptation of *Dracula,* with Bela Lugosi.

1930   Death of Lon Chaney.

1931   *Dracula* (USA). Tod Browning's film adaptation of the play, with Bela Lugosi.

1931   *Frankenstein* (USA). James Whale's masterpiece, starring Boris Karloff.

1932   *Freaks* (USA). Tod Browning's "antihorror" horror film on circus freaks.

1932   *Vampyr* (France). Dreyer's tri-national masterpiece very loosely based on Stoker's *Dracula.*

1933   *King Kong* (USA). The prototype of special-effects monster films, with Fay Wray.

1935   *The Bride of Frankenstein* (USA). Tod Browning's somewhat tongue-in-cheek sequel to *Frankenstein*, with Karloff and Elsa Lanchester as the "bride."

1941   *Dr. Jekyll and Mr. Hyde* (USA). Victor Fleming's remake of Mamoulian's 1932 version. Starring Spencer Tracy and Ingrid Bergman.

1946   Death of Lionel Atwill, a key supporting actor in numerous horror films.

1951   Death of Val Lewton, producer of *The Cat People, I Walked with a Zombie,* and others.

1953   *House of Wax* (USA). First horror film in 3-D.

1955   *Godzilla* (Japan). The first of a long series of Japanese monster films.

1956   Death of Bela Lugosi.

1957   *The Curse of Frankenstein* (Great Britain). Launched Hammer Films as the successor to Universal as specialists in the horror genre.

1960   *The House of Usher* (USA). The first of Roger Corman's long line of adaptations of the macabre stories of Edgar Allan Poe.

1960   *Psycho* (USA). Hitchcock's prototype of the psychological thriller in the horror genre.

1968   *Night of the Living Dead* (USA). Underground cult film on zombies, now emerging above ground.

1969   Death of Boris Karloff.

THE HORROR DOMAIN

Ghoulies and Ghosties
by CURTIS HARRINGTON

The ability of the camera to present hallucinatory or supernatural phenomena was one of the first discoveries made by the earliest creators of cinema; indeed, the most outstanding of the early innovators, Méliès, presented a great variety of supernatural visions in his "magically arranged scenes." His films abounded in fairies and ghosts and powerful magicians. But because of the camera's more obvious talent for objective recording, the cinema, as it subsequently grew and as it still is made use of to-day, has largely served to reconstruct a very earthbound reality. In the United States the financial failure of a "fantasy" is considered almost certain, and so they are rarely attempted. The few successes (the *Topper* series, *Here Comes Mr. Jordan*) have mostly been whimsical, using the tricks made possible by the varied mechanical resources of the camera for laughter rather than mystery or awe; while films that started out seriously, like *The Uninvited*, usually lost their supernatural convictions halfway through and dwindled away into obvious comedy. In Europe, ghosts have been the subject of more genuine wit, as in René Clair's *The Ghost Goes West* and, more notably, Max Ophuls' *La Tendre Ennemie*, in which three ghosts—of a woman's husband and her two lovers—sit on a chandelier during a dinner party given to celebrate the engagement of the woman's daughter to an old man she does not love. They finally alter the course of her life by persuading her to elope with someone else.

The fact of the matter is that camera "magic," despite its slickness and theoretically real and solid appearance, is a fairly obvious thing; a man double-exposed so that he can be seen through looks not so much as we imagine a ghost might, but rather as a man double-

From Sight and Sound *21* (*April–June, 1952*): *157–61. Copyright* © *1952 by the British Film Institute. Reprinted by permission of the author.*

exposed. The latter effect used to-day is really only a formal device; we say, "there is a figure double-exposed, which means he is supposed to be a ghost." But we are not convinced; there is not truly a "suspension of disbelief," so we can hardly be captured even momentarily by the illusion, as we may so often be by the dramatic pull of a situation, or the dramatic reality of a character. The mechanical fact stares us in the face, and that is all.

During the 'teens and 'twenties the supernatural was treated in many ways, perhaps most often by the Germans, whose love of mysticism is reflected strongly in their cinema. There were supernatural elements in all of the early German legend films, such as Galeen's *The Golem,* von Gerlach's *Chronicle of the Grieshuus,* and Lang's *Siegfried.* The first contained a remarkably well handled sequence of the summoning of a demon according to the kabbala; the second —about the ghosts of two tormented lovers who rescue a child from scheming relatives in a Gothic castle—had Lil Dagover appearing in double exposure rather often as a warning spirit; and the third showed Siegfried's borrowed cloak of invisibility in all its practicality. The Germans also produced the first film version of Bram Stoker's classic vampire story, *Dracula,* although it was considerably rewritten by its scenarist, Henrik Galeen, made into a kind of old German legend and retitled *Nosferatu.* In this the director, F. W. Murnau, used with, to contemporary eyes, rather crude but charming effect, the device of speeded action to show the supernatural strength of the master of the castle. A genuine sense of the macabre was conveyed by this, in combination with a general air of mystery and the frightening make-up of Max Schreck as the bloodthirsty count. Here double exposure, that obvious and so dangerous device for showing the supernatural, was used toward the end of the film to convey the death of the latter; and as a commentary rather than sustained image (the figure dissolves into the air, disappearing altogether) its use was, even, effective.

About this same time in Hollywood the French director Maurice Tourneur, who had established a reputation for his pictorial style (not, one suspects, without considerable help from his art directors) during the late 'teens, produced Maeterlink's *The Blue Bird* (1921) and a fantasy called *Prunella* (1922), about a strange little girl brought up in a strange house by three grim aunts and two prim maids, who kept her from the outside world, but could not prevent her falling in love with a pierrot. In these the fantastic effects were achieved as they are on the stage (both were originally plays), mechanically rather than by trickery of the camera. After *The Four Horsemen* and its misty apocalyptic visions, Rex Ingram included a fantastic and terrifying dream sequence in *The Conquering Power* (1921), and the morality tale within his *Trifling Women* (1923) was an elaborate and macabre vampiric love story in the tradition of Huysman's *A Rebours*. There were fantastic episodes also in Ingram's *Mare Nostrum* (1926), and in his version of Maugham's novel *The Magician* (1927), with its central figure drawn from the late Aleister Crowley, which contained an orgiastic dream sequence concerning Pan. Other American directors during the 'twenties dealt with the fantastic from time to time as their story material demanded, but Tourneur and Ingram were perhaps the two most consistently interested in using films to present fantasy rather than reality.

It is difficult to place where the fantastic "horror" film, as a genre, became established; but in America certainly the actor Lon Chaney, in a series of alarming make-ups, helped to establish the tradition. However, it was not until the coming of sound, and, incidentally, the stock market crash, that the fantastic horror film became a staple Hollywood commodity. With *Dracula* (1930) directed by Tod Browning (he had earlier directed Lon Chaney in *The Unholy Three*), and James Whale's *Frankenstein* (1931), the genre was definitely launched. These were followed by, to name a few of the most outstanding, *The Werewolf of London* (1933), *The White Zombie* (1933): *The Mark of the Vampire* (Browning; 1933), with Professor Zalen, an expert on vampire lore, solving the mystery of vampiric attacks on a young girl in a derelict castle: *The Mummy* (1934) and *The Black Cat* (1934), based on the Edgar Allan Poe story: *The Devil Doll* (Browning, 1934), about a French scientist who could reduce living creatures to a sixth of their normal size: and *The Bride of Frankenstein* (James Whale, 1935), with its splendid climax of a bride being created for the monster during a raging thunderstorm at night, the bride (Elsa Lanchester) being brought to life inside a bottle but horrified, upon emerging, at her intended mate. James Whale, a British stage director imported to America, brought to his films a fine sense of Gothic terror in the English tradition, as well as an irascible though perhaps less evident sense of humor. Tod Browning's work was less distinguished, though *The Mark of the Vampire* has its following. Its illusion, however, is quite destroyed when the ending of the film reveals the whole story to have been a carefully staged hoax.

Edmund Wilson has remarked how the popularity of the ghost and horror story in literature rises during times of outward stress in society, and certainly the vogue for this genre of film follows the same pattern. By 1939 the horror film had almost ceased to be produced, and it was only during the subsequent war that it was revived by the late Val Lewton, a producer then at R.K.O. studios. During the time the popularity of the horror film had declined in inverse proportion to the gradual revival of economic strength and prosperity, it had not only been produced less often but became exclusively "B," or low budget, second feature work. Thus, when Val Lewton produced his first film of this type, *The Cat People* (1943), it was at the customary low cost. To everyone's surprise, it had an amazing success as a first-class feature, and took in a great deal of money. It was, however, something slightly new.

The story of *The Cat People* is of Irena (Simone Simon), descendant of a race who, at times of emotional crisis, could turn into cats. Her psychiatrist is skeptical, but a few days later his body, bloody and clawed, is found in her apartment. Lewton had observed that the power of the camera as an instrument to generate suspense in an audience lies not in its power to reveal, but its power to suggest; that what takes place just off-screen in the audience's imagination, the terror of *waiting* for the final revelation, not the seeing of it, is the most powerful dramatic stimulus toward tension and fright. Moreover, where a fantastic subject is concerned, in order to obtain the modern audience's "suspension of disbelief," they must be kept in suspense as to the exact nature of whatever phenomenon they are to be frightened by—and this center of suggested terror must be surrounded by human, understandable people in realistic though possibly exotic surroundings. Thus the predicament of the girl in *The Cat People,* her growing realization of her impulses, was made direct and real. Upon this formula Lewton produced a number of horror fantasies, made by directors now well-known: Jacques Tourneur (*The Cat People*), the son of Maurice Tourneur, Mark Robson and Robert Wise. The films dealt with zombies in Haiti (*I Walked with a Zombie*), devil worship (*The Seventh Victim*), a child's imagination (*The Curse of the Cat People*), the living dead (*Isle of the Dead*), and an especially macabre murderer (*The Leopard Man*). Robert Louis Stevenson's *The Body Snatchers* was also imaginatively filmed with Lewton as producer and Wise as director, as was a story based on Hogarth's drawings of *Bedlam* (Mark Robson).

Though made independently on a very low budget, a film that de-

serves mention along with the Lewton product is Frank Wysbar's
The Strangler of the Swamp. Wysbar, who directed *Anna und Eliza-
beth* and *Fahrmann Maria* during the early 'thirties in Germany,
came to Hollywood as a refugee during the war, and made several
rather curious low-budget films. *The Strangler of the Swamp*, the
only fantasy among them, dealt with the malign ghost of a man
unjustly hanged in a Southern swampland. Although the treatment
was on the whole realistic, it contained suggestions of German expressionism, and succeeded in evoking with considerable effect the
mist-laden, spirit-haunted country in which the strange story takes
place.

These have been the most interesting horror fantasies produced
in Hollywood; one must record, for other reasons, the films made
by Universal Studios during the war years. Whereas Val Lewton attempted within commercial restrictions to do something new and
imaginative, all the films produced at Universal (a studio famous as
the home of "horror" film, though in the early 'thirties both Paramount and M.G.M. probably produced an equal share) were life-
less repetitions of ancient penny-dreadful formulas. A whole series
of crudely ridiculous films were made, exploiting some famous originals—*House of Frankenstein, Son of Dracula, The Wolf Man, The
Spider Woman, The Mummy's Ghost*—and the final death agony
of James Whale's originally marvellous creation, *Abbott and Costello
Meet Frankenstein*. Columbia Studios' product of this type was only
very occasionally better; Edward Dmytryk's *The Devil Commands*
(1942) built to a genuinely frightening climax, but it was weighted
by a dully concocted story—a grief-stricken husband tries to contact
the spirit of his dead wife through a brain machine, with the aid of
a weird medium.

With the end of the war the popularity of horror films quickly
diminished, so that since 1947 there have been few, if any, produced.
Even Universal gave them up. Recently a new type of fantasy has
come to the screen in the form of "science-fiction" films, which "explain" the supernatural in terms of science and in which mysterious
happenings are generated by machines rather than human beings.
At least one of these, however, proves to be simply a modern version
of Mary Shelley's old morality thriller, *Frankenstein; or A Modern
Prometheus*. In *The Thing*, horror and suspense are produced during the first part by only suggesting verbally the nature of "The
Thing," a monstrous vegetable-man from another planet, but as
soon as he is seen, fully clothed and looking altogether like Karloff's

creation of "The Monster" in *Frankenstein,* the illusion of horror that has been built up is quickly dispelled. By now we have seen this creature too often; we produced him on this earth, and we expect another planet to be able to think up something different.

This brief outline of, primarily, the supernatural horror film may serve to indicate what has, in the main, been done with the genre; now this varied, sometimes remarkable, but relatively unimaginative output must be contrasted with one truly serious and brilliant creation, Carl-Theodor Dreyer's *Vampyr.* Dreyer's work, besides, is particularly interesting in this respect, since he is the only outstanding film director to have used the supernatural more than once to express a personal outlook on life. Produced in France during 1930 and 1931, about the same time as *Dracula* and *Frankenstein,* Dreyer's *Vampyr* was released in 1932, at the time the vogue for horror films, at least in America, was mounting quickly. The film was premiered in Berlin, and although it was dubbed (easily and effectively, for there was very little dialogue) in both French and English it had little success outside of Germany, where its mystic quality seems to have been appreciated.

Inspiration for the story of *Vampyr* is credited to Sheridan le Fanu's *In a Glass Darkly.* A reading of this collection shows that only one story bears any relationship to the film, and that only vaguely, the tale of a vampire, "Carmilla." Rather than from any particular literary basis, the film seems more to have developed from its settings (it was shot entirely on location in various deserted buildings), in which were placed a certain number of rather extraordinary characters living out their destiny in the shadow of a human vampire. Briefly, the continuity reveals the arrival of a young man at an inn beside a lake, where, during the night, a man enters his room and leaves with him a sealed package, with instructions that it is to be opened upon his death. The next morning the young man investigates a strange building where shadows dance eternally, and visits an odd little doctor at his office where he meets also an old lady (who is the vampire). Presently he arrives at a chateau whose master is the man who had come to his room at the inn. The man has two daughters, Gisèle and Léone, and two servants. Léone is ill, having been attacked by the vampire. Suddenly and mysteriously the girls' father is shot, and the young man opens the package he had been given earlier. In it is *The Book of Vampires,* which relates the vampire legend, and tells how the vampire can be destroyed. Léone leaves her bed and is discovered in the woods surrounding the chateau, attacked once again by the vampire. The doctor is called to administer a transfusion, and the young man gives his blood. Later the young man's *doppelgänger*, in a dream, experiences his enclosure in a coffin by the doctor and the vampire, and he is carried toward the cemetery. Then, awakening, he goes to the cemetery, where the old servant opens the tomb of the vampire and drives a stake through her heart; she turns to a skeleton, and Léone sits up in bed, released. With the power of the vampire no longer sustaining him the doctor runs away in panic, and is trapped by the old servant in a mill where the machines bury him slowly in a shower of white flour. The young man and Gisèle, meanwhile, ride in a boat through the misty lake and at last, arriving on the other side, walk into a forest illumined by the sun.

As with any film of style and value, a bare recounting of the plot (I prefer in this case the word "continuity," since it sounds more sequential, in a filmic sense, than constructed, in a literary sense) does not give one any idea of what the film is actually like; the structure of *Vampyr* is based more upon imagery than idea. Ebbe Neergaard, in his *Carl Dreyer,* one of the British Film Institute Index Series, tells how the script called for the doctor to die by sinking into a bog of mud. Yet when Dreyer came by chance upon a plaster-works where everything was covered with a fine white dust, he realized the image-requirement for the film was that the doctor die in whiteness, and so an old flour mill, where the doctor could be trapped in the cage where the bags are filled, was chosen for the film. The earlier sequences, then, were carefully photographed by Maté to match, in style, the final image material. The first arrival of the young man at the inn is suffused in a late afternoon grayness. The sequence of his discovery of the building filled with mysterious shadows is in tones of white and gray. The succeeding exteriors—the young man's arrival at the chateau, his walk to the cemetery, and Léone's encounter with the vampire, are all extremely diffused so as to give a kind of preternatural mist-effect. There is no sun in the film until the final moment.

What is especially striking about *Vampyr* is that light and shadow become more than just contributors to a consistent style; they serve as dynamic participants in the story unfolded. Dreyer recognized immediately the principle that Val Lewton applied to his series of films dealing with the supernatural twelve years later, that you must only suggest horror; you cannot show it, or at least, if you do, it must only be momentarily, for you cannot sustain it. It is the audience's own imagination, skillfully probed, that provides, out of its well of unconscious fear, all the horror necessary.

In what are perhaps the most uncanny and terrifying moments of *Vampyr,* only a wild inexplicable play of light and shadow is seen; but the terror of the malevolent supernatural force is brilliantly conveyed. One of the most effective of these moments is when the doctor, after having given the blood transfusion, leaves Léone's room and the young man runs after him, only to reach the head of the stairs and find them quite empty; then we hear an abrupt crash and see the shadows cast by the staircase railings jerking crazily around on the walls of the stairwell. Throughout the film all such moments, actions communicated by purely filmic means, are left an unexplained part of the general uncanny atmosphere. We are transported to the heart of a battle between ancient evil and the young, the pure in heart, taking place in a land convincingly haunted, where anything may at any moment happen and does.

One cannot properly divorce *Vampyr* from Dreyer's other work, as it must be considered partly, along with these, as an expression of his personality. Certainly Dreyer is one of the very few directors of whom this may be fairly and safely said; no major studio chose the script of *Vampyr,* and there was no "front office" to interfere in any way with the execution. This seems to be fairly true also of *Jeanne d'Arc* and *Day of Wrath*—the former made immediately before *Vampyr,* the other twelve years after it. Seen in perspective the three films make up a kind of trilogy; they all bear definite affinities of theme, style and content. Each presents a struggle between good and evil, age and youth, and in each there is an intense concern, almost amounting to obsession, with the *act* of death; in *Jeanne d'Arc* the progress toward death by fire; in *Vampyr* the death of the head of the manor, then the true death of the living dead and of the doctor and his assistant, and, during the whole of the film, the delicate suspension near death of Léone; and finally, in *Day of Wrath,* the death, again by fire, of the old lady declared a witch, the death of the parson, and Anne's acceptance, at the end of the film, of her identity as a witch, indicating surely the death to follow. In all three of the films the conquering of this miasma of death and old age is shown as only a temporary thing—a gesture of St. Joan's; the young lovers' idyll in *Day of Wrath*; and although in *Vampyr* the young man and Gisèle escape, at the end, they never really seem to emerge from the land of phantoms. Another recurrent figure that one notices in many of Dreyer's films is the powerful, often malevolent old lady. She was not, of course, seen in *Jeanne d'Arc* (where certain of the older priests might be said to have taken her place), but she was portrayed with humor very early in Dreyer's career as *The Parson's Widow* (1920) and she mastered the tyrant in *Thou Shalt Honor Thy Wife* (1925). In *Vampyr* she becomes the ancient, powerful living dead creature of the title, and in *Day of Wrath* she is two forces —the narrow, suspicious old mother of the parson, and Marte, the old lady accused as a witch who goes to her death uttering dire curses against those who have condemned her.

As remarkable as the photographic treatment of *Vampyr* is the sound. Wolfgang Zeller composed a score that for suggestivity has seldom been equalled, perhaps because there have been no other films since then requiring quite such imaginative work. It is not, of course, music that could be divorced from the film. The dialogue is very sparse and effectively pointed, as when, after giving the blood transfusion to Léone, the young man complains (he is resting in an adjoining room) to the doctor, who peeks out at him from behind the door of Léone's room, that he is losing blood. *"Don't be silly,"* the doctor replies very slowly, *"your blood is in here."* Sound effects are also used with the utmost suggestivity. One remembers the inexplicable noises heard in the doctor's office, distant barkings and cryings, which make the young man ask the doctor if there are children or dogs on the premises. *"There are no children or dogs here,"* the doctor replies. When, from a subjective viewpoint, we experience with the young man our enclosure in a coffin, there is unique horror as we hear the close grinding of the screws into the coffin-lid, and experience the splutter of a match struck to light a candle placed on the coffin-lid by the vampire who, in doing so, peers at us intently.

The last sequence of the film is very formally constructed and gives us, I believe, insight into Dreyer's creative method, one which always tends toward formal control, especially when he is dealing with incident and outward movement rather than people. Here we have the escape of the young couple counter-pointed with the death of the doctor in the flour mill. The sequence is cross-cut, so that at one moment we see and hear the machinery rhythmically grinding out its white death, and the next we see the young couple gliding slowly on the mist-covered lake, the image being accompanied by a slow sustained note of music. This combination of shots is repeated in alternation until the couple get out of the boat and go into the sunlit forest. The very final shot is a close-up of the white turning gears of the flour mill machinery; their movement slows, and at last stops. Fade out; we have reached the end of the adventure. The construction and the image-material here employed is perfectly cinematographic; the meaning communicated is melodramatic incident abstracted into a pattern of time, space and sound. The sum of this design toward a conclusion becomes greater than the actions of its parts; it brings to an end not only the adventure we have had (for it has been *our* adventure as much as the protagonist's), but encloses the film perfectly in its own uniqueness as the sole cinematic work that shakes us with its revelations of the terrors that still haunt us in the deep and unknown places of the human psyche.

Rough Beasts Slouching
by FRANK McCONNELL

"What will you do if the people you knew
Were the plastic that melted and the
chromium, too?"

—FRANK ZAPPA

One of the minor developments of taste of the last decade has been the accession of the horror film to that kind of demi-monde respectability the academic mind confers also on the detective thriller, the Gothic novel, and Carl Orff. For a long time now, collegiate "great film" festivals have been likely to include, besides *Intolerance,* and *The Treasure of Sierra Madre,* Bela Lugosi's 1931 *Dracula* or the classic 1933 *King Kong,* or any of the numerous specimens turned out by Universal Studios before the outbreak of World War II. Critics like Harold Bloom and Susan Sontag have mapped out the uses the adverting mind might make of such productions: Bloom for their socio-psychological import, and Miss Sontag for the naïveté of their "pure form." Carlos Clarens' *Illustrated History of the Horror Film* is a complete, if pedestrian, survey of the genre. The final intellectual baptism of the horror film was performed, of course, by Miss Sontag in the essays, "Notes on Camp" and "The Imagination of Disaster," but it was a baptism of doubtful efficacy. The whimsical aesthetic of "camp," after all, is—as Miss Sontag herself makes clear—one which depends as much upon the poise of the beholder as upon the nature of the object. With minds less capacious and finely tuned than her own, the active delight of the critic is too likely to relax into the passive enjoyment of the afficionado. That a good number of intelligent people dig Dracula is clear: that many are

Appeared originally as "Rough Beast Slouching: A Note on Horror Movies," in Kenyon Review, *No. 1 (1970), 109–20. Copyright © 1970 by Kenyon College. Reprinted by permission of Kenyon College and the author.*

trying to make efficient sense of him as more than a symptom of social pathology is less than apparent.

Not that the maintenance of an academic demi-monde is itself
reprehensible; I am only questioning whether the horror movie
really belongs there. Academics, and especially literary critics, like
and probably need some sort of safe imaginative suburb where they
can exercise the powers of attention and analysis that belong to their
craft, but in a spirit of free play and measured irresponsibility. The
strain and high seriousness involved in working with James or Milton, and the nagging, unadmitted tedium which is a minor byprod-
uct of imaginative greatness, are things that work themselves off
easily and without too great a sense of betrayal in the fiction of
Dashiell Hammett or the complexities of pro-football strategy. The
difficulty is that the continuum of art is less compartmentalized than
the hierarchical mind of the critic: the suburbs of imagination frequently turn out to be more crucial than imagined to the balance
of the center. Robbe-Grillet's comments, in *For a New Novel*, on
the innate existentialism of detective literature should make it impossible to read Hammett with relaxed inattention; and even tele-
vised professional football, as discussed by Marshall McLuhan in
Understanding Media, takes on a high significance in his half-con-
vincing system. The act of criticism tends, properly, to its own un-
willed exhaustion-through-articulation; and, since it permanently
lags behind the unselfconscious process of culture itself, it is involved in a sustained shock of recognition—the recognition that
what seemed adventitious is in fact nontrivial.

The horror film is, I think, a remarkable instance of submerged
value, precisely because that value has come to consciousness and
full articulation not through the development of critical intelligence but through the development of art itself. The difficulty of
reading a page of William S. Burroughs' *Nova Express,* listening to
a song like Frank Zappa's *Who Are the Brain Police?,* or seeing
a film like Conrad Rooks's remarkable *Chappaqua* is a difficulty
anticipated by and implicit in the structure of *Them!* (1954) or
Invasion of the Body Snatchers (1956). To put that difficulty in its
most tiresomely familiar form, it is the problem of the demise of
liberal humanism, the advent of the art of dehumanization. And,
like most clichés, the "art of dehumanization" is not an inaccurate,
but only an unexplored, term. Critics who, like Leslie Fiedler or
George Steiner, accuse Burroughs or Robbe-Grillet of eliminating
man from the purview of the novel are commenting on a process

which includes also the transition from the debased humanity of film vampires in the '30s to the chilling inhumanity of the plant- and insect-monsters of the '50s and '60s.

I have designedly mentioned only American-made horror movies to this point, because the horror movie as a genre is, of course, distinctively American. This is so partly because of sheer plenitude of production, but also for rather more subtle reasons. The peculiarly American sense of art as mass medium which leads from Whitman through Hollywood to Roy Lichtenstein allies itself, in the case of prepackaged horror, with impulses more apparently imaginative. *The Cabinet of Dr. Caligari* (1920) is scrupulously experimental art, and recent British and European chillers are usually bald importations of Yankee industry, like Coca-Cola or the $2.00 transistor. But with Universal's *Dracula* and *Frankenstein* in 1931 a distinctive national mythography and commodity are born simultaneously.

Dracula and *Frankenstein* establish the form with overwhelmingly crude authority. But besides setting its limits, they also indicate the possible complexities available to the constricted genre: complexities the more striking since they are almost totally of the surface. Both movies are translations not only of novels into film but of English Romanticism into a profoundly Americanized mental landscape. They are translations, that is, in the sense D. H. Lawrence described the compulsion of classic American writers to translate and revalue the inherited burden of European culture. In the case of *Dracula,* the earlier of the two films, this translation is almost too complete. Based not on Bram Stoker's novel but on a successful stage version of the novel which had just completed its American tour, the film is basically a succession of stage scenes, from a proscenium-arch point of view, and employs surprisingly few of the closeups, dissolves, and special effects which have since become stock-in-trade for the vampire movie. And, of course, the plot of the movie itself, insofar as there is a plot at all, is one of a special kind of translation: Count Dracula, having exhausted the populace of his native Transylvania, has himself transported in his coffin to England, where the blood is fresh and his existence is unknown. But the "England" of *Dracula* is transparently a New England, even to the accents of most of the major characters. With barely proleptic symbolism, Bela Lugosi's Dracula is the Roger Chillingworth of Lend-Lease: the strange, suspiciously epicene emissary from that Europe which had hardly been suspected, and whose sheer presence jolts us from our comfortable insularity. The invocation of Hawthorne is not inappropriate: for what Dracula comes to destroy is an insularity not primarily of space but of history. In one of his finest speeches in the film, Lugosi's Dracula says to the scholar who has just unmasked his vampirism: "For a man who has lived not even one lifetime, Van Helsing, you are very wise." What gives this line its resonance is not the conflict between the Count and Van Helsing (who is also Transylvanian), but the tension between the *impersonated* mind of Dracula and the collective mind of producer and audience which gives him his existence: between imaginary toad and real garden. The date, 1931, is important: Dracula carries the conscious weight of cumulative history, of more than one lifetime, into a society that was just making a public discovery of the closure of the future. He is, again, a translated image, borrowed from an Irish novelist and two English playwrights: but the very borrowing constitutes an excitingly crude attempt to imagine the alien-ness of history. As such, his true roots are Hawthorne's Chillingworth and the symbol-obsessed Reverend Hooper, and even more those monumentally defeated Europeans of the late James, whose defeat is finally not only their own but that of their creator to imagine them triumphant. As the Prince says to Maggie Verver in *The Golden Bowl*: "One is made up of the history, the doings, the marriages, the crimes, the follies, the boundless *bêtises* of other people." It is a knowledge Maggie cannot ultimately bear, and her attempt to bear it destroys the Prince, just as the compulsion to imagine Dracula necessitates his interminable redestructions in the American film. The clash of time-senses comes across brilliantly in the movie, due primarily to the exquisite mincing grace of Lugosi's movements. Where everyone else walks and gestures with "normal" theatricality, he choreographs himself in slow-motion.

If Dracula is a nightmare-extension of Hawthorne and James, Frankenstein, the more successful if less inherently interesting film, has the same kind of relationship to the archetype of self-constituting omnipotence—that archetype which *is* the "Walt Whitman" created by Walt Whitman. The process is encapsulated by D. H. Lawrence, eight years before the filming of *Frankenstein*:

> Post-mortem effects?
> But what of Walt Whitman?
> The "good grey poet."
> Was he a ghost, with all his physicality?
> The good grey poet.
> Post-mortem effects. Ghosts.

The expansive self, which assimilates and verbalizes the entire range of its phenomena, is transformed, with inevitable psychic economy, into the spectral, mocking shadow of its expansion. Whitman's own "As I Ebb'd" and "The Sleepers" are testaments of this dialectic. As is *Frankenstein*. The primary resemblances between the Boris Karloff movie and Mary Shelley's novel, of course, end with the title: but there is a more subtle analogic relationship which goes far to explain the profound impact *Frankenstein* was to have on the future of American movie-making. Harold Bloom has convincingly interpreted Mary Shelley's novel as an inversion of the Blakean and Shelleyan myth of the integration of the self: at the end of the book, monster and creator pursue each other across the arctic waste in a grotesque parody of the integrative triumph of *Prometheus Unbound* III where self (the male Prometheus) and emanation (the female Asia) celebrate their milennial epithalamium. But as Whitman's version of the integrated imagination was both more ambitious and more omnivorously assimilative than either Blake's or Shelley's, so the inversion of that myth, the movie monster, is both more crudely materialistic and more infantile than Mrs. Shelley's articulate and anguished creation. In the case of *Frankenstein,* unlike that of Dracula, the star is clearly too good for his vehicle. Karloff's miraculous pantomime—he came from the same music-hall tradition as Chaplin—almost spoils the sense of dumb malevolence which is the tenor of the film. For the tension between the intelligent, nearly neurotic Dr. Frankenstein of Colin Clive and the monster he creates conceals a phenomenology known to Whitman and to Fitzgerald's Nick Carraway: that creative consciousness controls its object, but exhausts itself in the act of controlling, finally to become as dull and insensate as the object-world itself. Even the creation of the monster in the movie *Frankenstein* is not effected by the near-alchemy of the English novel, but by an absurdly reductive production line of anatomical bits and pieces: the process which made possible Ford, paperbacks, and napalm.

Between them, these movies mark the limits of most later horror films. They are not themselves "archetypal" in any comprehensible use of that word, but they were something more immediately important: successful. And, with a respect for the ingredients of success more astringent than any aesthetic concern for genre-convention, Hollywood produced a series of films which are essentially permutations and combinations of the original elements. The Wolf-Man series, for example, as played by Lon Chaney, Jr., involves only a collapsing of the articulate, well-meaning creator and the compulsive, brutish monster of the Frankenstein-form into a single, tormented individual (quite forgetting that lykanthropy is traditionally a prerogative of vampires). And a well-done "spectacular" of 1945, *House of Dracula,* includes all three figures, Dracula, Frankenstein's monster, and the Wolf-Man—but kept apart from each other throughout the film with a carefulness reminiscent of the isolation of major figures in traditional allegory. In fact, the separation of the two major monster-types achieves the status almost of a structural principle during the '30s and '40s. Frankenstein may meet the Wolf-Man, as in the disappointing 1943 movie; but he never really confronts Dracula, in spite of what would appear to be the box-office blessing invoked by such a union.

The reason for the quarantine I have already partly indicated: it is a combination of commercial and imaginative wisdom, both probably conscious and each nearly indistinguishable from the other. Thinking of the two great fiends and their implications, one is reminded again of Lawrence who, discussing Poe, defines the dual rhythm of "American art-activity": "1. A disintegrating and sloughing of the old consciousness. 2. The forming of a new consciousness underneath." But this rhythm, though dual, is diastole and systole of a single cultural dynamic: one movement present by implication or anticipation in the other. And the two monsters, Dracula and Frankenstein, are the fabricated negatives of that rhythm. The vampire is the "old consciousness," not sloughed off but resurrected to drain the blood of the new; and the artificial man is the "new man" of Edenic materialism, but with the brain of a killer. Each monster is present in the other, both by the mechanics of mythography and by their permanent association in the popular mind: but their explicit combination is a kind of imaginative overkill, an image of terror which pushes the horror film, already innately and perilously ludicrous, over the edge of absurdity. And, in fact, the only movie, to my knowledge, in which we see Dracula cooperating with the Frankenstein monster in planned malevolence is the 1948 comedy, *Abbott and Costello Meet Frankenstein,* where the plan is to invoke the horror in order to laugh it off.

What Lawrence did not—and could not allow himself to—grasp about this dual rhythm is its high quotient of factitiousness. The dark gods of consciousness that Lawrence found in Hawthorne and Melville are indisputably there, but, as Richard Poirier has perceptively demonstrated, they are there in a manifestation eminently *constructed.* This sense of deliberately obvious artifice in the American impulse to project "a world elsewhere" provides one important transition between the frankly—if problematically—apocalyptic imagination of Romanticism and the self-parodistic celebration of the arbitrary which is probably the central "modern" imaginative tradition. That tradition may be, and is, called either "existential" or "analytic," depending upon which side of the Channel the critic's sensibilities inhabit: but I think "analysis" and the invocation of Wittgenstein are helpful, since writers like Burroughs, Barth, and Pynchon are involved with the velleities and treacheries not only of the object-world but of the medium of language itself. One of Wittgenstein's favorite riddles, in *The Brown Book* and the *Lectures on Aesthetics,* is the little drawing:

which the observer immediately describes as a drawing of a face. But, Wittgenstein asks, is it that we recognize it as a face because of some inner, imagined form of "face" we compare it with, or "rather that we let the picture sink into our mind and make a mould there"? It is a crucially symptomatic question. In much the same manner, one can imagine the John Barth of *Giles Goat-Boy* asking: do the archetypes of "hero" and "action" we think we bear in our minds and our culture, not to mention our conventions of "story" and "ending," really exist there, or are they simply readings, ways of seeing a given series of words, which make no innate sense at all and can therefore be summarily and thoroughly invented? The action is much like Wittgenstein's forcing us to look at the face until we really *see* only the arbitrary grouping of marks on paper out of which our "meaning" is built. Those readers who object to the "obviousness" of the allegory in *Giles Goat-Boy,* like those who object to the "chaos" of Burroughs' fold-in technique in *Nova Express,* barely—and therefore totally—miss the point. It is precisely the outrageous surface of such novels, at once terrifyingly complex and almost entirely without depth, which gives them their characteristic mode of existence. They constitute a firm denial that the Word has any dimensions other than those of the *trompe-l'oeil,* and simultaneously the insistence that, for human concerns, this is enough.

It is an aesthetic—perhaps an epistemology—which pertains with equal accuracy to the horror films I have been discussing. Dracula and Frankenstein are nightmare-inversions whose roots go back to the masters of nineteenth-century American literature, but the principal ingredient of their nightmarishness is precisely the bland theatricality, the decadent ease, with which they establish themselves as such bad dreams. I am speaking now, of course, of a response to these movies which may be that of neither the audience nor the makers, but nevertheless a response they generally seem capable of bearing. It is, in fact, the eminently *cosmetic* nature of Lugosi's Dracula and Karloff's monster which raises them to a high level of art: accidentally, perhaps, but in the grammar of Barth or Burroughs—or Wittgenstein or E. M. Cioran—the distinction between accidental and planned art is a trivial one. They are marked by a monumental technical simplemindedness, and by a capriciousness of plot construction which, in its very banality, achieves a unified effect of overwhelmingly weary poetry. The two pieces of music heard throughout *Dracula,* for example, are *Swan Lake* and the Overture to *Der Meistersinger*: ludicrous choices for a sepulchral score, which yet, in the context of the movie, and in their spotty performance by the Universal Studio Orchestra, do support the roughed horror of Lugosi's vampire. The general tone of response is set with unusual self-consciousness in the most famous sequence from *The Mummy* (1932). As the young American archaeologist, alone in his tent, is working on his notes, the recently exhumed mummy of Im-ho-tep begins slowly, horribly, to move out of his erect sarcophagus, and at the sight of the terrifying, and transparently, disguised features of Karloff, the archaeologist begins to laugh, crazily and mirthlessly, for what seems an interminable minute-and-a-half of screen time. It is laughter at the gratuitously terrible, the absurd *presence* of the horror-object itself. And the theme of *The Mummy* is also *Swan Lake.*

The horror film of the '30s and early '40s has, according to its dedicated fans, passed out of existence. The science-fiction products of the postwar era, with their atomic mutations or alien invaders, represent a different and less humanly recognizable version of the frightening: one appropriate to a post-Hiroshima age, but one inevitably degenerate from the films of the genre's heyday. Whatever the sense of debating the relative excellence of *The Bride of Frankenstein* and *The Fly*, this opinion misses the very real connection between earlier and later horror films. The venerable truism that what is more recognizably human is more terrifying to us is, of course, accurate as a generality: but in the specific case of the American horror movie it is exactly inverted. As I have said, what makes Dracula and Frankenstein, and their progeny, really horrifying to us is their banality, the obvious and arbitrary theatricality of their existence. No less than the pre-Reich Munich of Mann's *Doktor Faustus* or Kurt Weill's acid lyricism, they anticipate the systematically nonchalant dehumanization of Treblinka (with dances organized among the inmates tagged for death), and the programmed cataclysm of the Manhattan Project (with Fermi bringing the first atomic pile to critical mass underneath the University of Chicago). And their precise aura of cliché'd evil is not supplanted by the giant insect mutants of the '50s, but in fact develops naturally into them.

There is even a continuity of technique. The classic horror film, I have indicated, has no "depth." One manifestation of this negative quality is in the arrangement of camera angles. With surprisingly few exceptions, these films maintain the point of view of a neutral third observer: one seldom sees the monster from the point of view of the victim or the victim from the point of view of the monster. The only remarkable exception to this, that I know of, is the 1953 film *It Came from Outer Space*, in which the monster- and victim-eye perspectives are at least partly occasioned by the 3-D process in which the film was originally made. The effect of the third-person point of view is literally to flatten the horror, to convert the potential depth-perception of panic into a two-dimensional tableau which, again, underscores the factitiousness of the monster. And in the postwar science-fiction products, this flatness of perception becomes all the more striking, since the monsters themselves are more deliberately alien. The giant insects of *Them!* or *Tarantula* (1955), or the alien of *The Thing* (1951), seem to demand a perspective and a plane of perception congruent to their degree of alienness. But the remorselessly plain camera angles of these movies insist on the same vantage for humans and monsters; and therefore inadvertently project flat visual equivalence between the "normal" and the freakish which is finally a devastating reduction of humanistic perception.

What I mean is best illustrated by a comparison. Anyone who has taught Kafka's *Metamorphosis* has probably encountered the discomfort students have about the matter of Gregor Samsa's size. It is difficult for them to imagine exactly how large a dung-beetle he really is. The difficulty, of course, is intimately involved with the center of Kafka's genius: in resolutely maintaining the point-of-view, and in fact the total phenomenology, of Gregor, he enforces the same pained uncertainty about the size of Gregor's insect-body that the reader, like everyone, feels about the dimensions, the "place," of his own body. The narrative of the story, in complex tension with its myth of dehumanization, is humanistic in the profound tradition of the European novel. An entirely different sense of transformation occurs, however, in the 1958 movie, *The Fly*. Here, a scientist experimenting with atomic matter-transportation finds his body horribly merged with that of a fly accidentally trapped in the transportation-chamber. Onto the fly's body is grafted the minuscule human head of the scientist, and onto the scientist's body is grafted the monstrous head of the fly. And in spite of the absurdly uninventive story-line of the movie, it manages a profound kind of shock: exactly because the flat, third-person camera angle imposes a tacit equivalence of inhuman and human which is the obverse of Kafka's vision. One is always quite sure of the size of fly-man and man-fly; and the disgusting horror of the film, and of its 1959 sequel, *Return of the Fly,* hinges on the innocently uncomplicated shuffling of human and bestial dimensions. There is, to be sure, an occasional multiple-lens, fly's-eye shot of a horrified victim; but the effect of this is not to enforce a depth-perspective but rather to underscore the arbitrary confusion of human and insect levels of perception. The technique, in fact, has the same aura of flat and designedly pointless reduplication as Andy Warhol's roughly contemporary silk-screen multiplications of photographs of Marilyn Monroe.

Monsters of the postwar period are predominantly either mutated varieties of plant or insect, rather than mammalian life—and even of mineral "life," in the 1957 *Monolith Monsters*—or alien, extraterrestrial and sometimes extragalactic invaders. The psychopolitical explanation of this change I have already indicated. But it is interesting to notice that the original, distinctively American duality of monster-forms still obtains in these films, with remarkable consistency. The insect and vegetable monsters are only more resolutely insensate, more unredeemable material inversions of the myth of imperial intelligence. To the creative imaginative question, "What is Grass?," they answer that it is an alien substance, a senseless and

perfect evolutionary success which can blindly destroy the evolutionary failure of a constitutive human consciousness. And the invariably humanoid and superarticulate aliens are a frequently
startling modification of the vampire motif. Their characteristic
mode of invasion is normally not weaponry but, following the
standard set by Robert Heinlein's famous novel, *The Puppet Masters,* some form of mental or metabolic possession, as in *Invasion of
the Body Snatchers* (1956). And the horror they project is also the
horror of incarnate history: but not the history of the Continental
past which will not die, rather the history of the uncontrollable,
atomic future in which man (for which these films always read, of
course, *homo Americanus*) finds himself displaced from total control
by "alien" worlds in the process of borning.

It is less than accidental, in this connection, that some of the most
successful postwar horror movies are Japanese. The Gargantuan,
city-wasting dinosaurs and insects of *Godzilla* (1955), *Varan the Un-
believable* (1958), and especially the wonderfully delicate *Mothra*
(1962) are neither vampire nor Frankenstein figures, but an odd
conflation of the two, a vision of the national archetypes from the
viewpoint of those archetypes' most signal victims. The "American-
ization" of Japan is itself one of the mutated flowers of Hiroshima;
and these slumbering, heraldic monsters, stung to outrage by (usually) atomic testing, are a half-dream of vengeance coupled with a
truly terrifying sense of self-annihilation. For it is always Tokyo, not
Chicago, that the dragon destroys, the production-line Ginza-strip
Tokyo of defeat and colonial transformation.

The elements of these films, as I have said, are an important
window onto what the tenor of our imaginative life has become
and is becoming. But they are more than simply supportive artifacts
for the cultural historian, preserved wind-harps of the post-Roman-
tic era. If it is difficult not to see in them reflections and nuances of
most of our major writers, it is sometimes impossible not to see in
some of our most brilliant writers the very pace and technique of
their visions. I quote from one such, William Burroughs describing
the Insect Planet of Minraud in *Nova Express*:

Controller of the Crab Nebula on a slag heap of smouldering
metal under the white hot sky channels all his pain into control
thinking—He is protected by heat and crab guards and the brains
armed now with The Blazing Photo from Hiroshima and Naga-
saki—The brains under his control are encased in a vast structure

of steel and crystal spinning thought patterns that control those galaxies thousand years ahead on the chessboard of virus screens and juxtaposition formulae—

Not only the images but the form itself belong to the world of the horror film and the tradition of imaginative reduction. Burroughs' monstrosities are metaphors not only for his "theme" but for his own process of creation: since his theme is precisely the limited chances available to the creative consciousness to save itself or the world it inhabits. His monsters are indifferently inhabitants of the galaxy or the brain-cage, as his narrative is indifferently an accidental chaos or a complex "juxtaposition formula."

The modern value of horror begins with M. G. Lewis and Blake, and the Romantic quest for a landscape appropriate to the expansive energies of the mind. And it is the closure of some circle that in this century, in the land Europe dreamed and discovered, that sense should have reversed itself into a search for the possibility of mind at all in the claustrophobic landscape of the object-universe. What Burroughs, Wittgenstein, and *Them!* unequally teach us is that the demons are ultimately from ourselves, and that what we may see as their Satanic grandeur is only, and more terribly, the flat reflection of our own dubious consciousness, with the added hope, in the best of our visions, that this may after all be enough to make us men.

The Pageantry of Death
by R. H. W. DILLARD

I suppose that all significant Western art, at least since the medieval period, has been directly concerned with the original fall of man and the consequent introduction of sin and death into the world. Certainly sin (or, if you prefer, human evil) and death must be the central concerns of any artist seriously involved with life; poetry can never be totally divorced from danger and still be of the highest order. The horror film is, at its best, as thoroughly and richly involved with the dark truths of sin and death as any art form has ever been, but its approach is that of parable and metaphor—an approach which enables it on occasion to achieve a metaphysical grandeur, but which also may explain why its failures are so very awful and indefensible.

Like a medieval morality play, the horror film deals with the central issue of Christian life—the struggle between the spirits of good and evil for the possession of man's immortal soul. In the morality play personified abstractions (Friendship, Knowledge, Evil Deeds, Good Deeds, Riches, Good Angel, Evil Angel, Death) argue for Vice and Virtue, and their actions free the soul to heaven or cast it down to hell. The plays were totally unrealistic and as completely serious, for they were attempts to image in the flesh on a stage the dreadful battle within the spirit between the divided forces of man's own nature—the love of God and other men versus the corrupt love of self and evil. To a medieval Catholic those plays were as true as art could ever be. The horror film is quite as unrealistic and, I believe, quite as concerned with the truth available to art.

If the morality play personified the elements of the human soul

From "Even a Man Who Is Pure at Heart," in W. R. Robinson, ed., Man and the Movies *(Baton Rouge: Louisiana State University Press, 1967), pp. 64–70. Copyright © 1967 by Louisiana State University Press. Reprinted by permission of the publisher. Title supplied.*

and set them forth for all to see in an instructive pageant, the horror
film personifies those very elements in a dark and beautiful dream
which, for all its vagueness and artificiality, is quite as instructive.
The horror film is a pageant of death, the death that breeds in all
things—entropy, mutability, and corruption. The morality play
taught the method of salvation to which a Christian should adhere
in order to pass through the temptations and sufferings of life to the
peace and joy of union with God; Death was the dangerous and unexpected bailiff who cast man before the final bar of justice, and
Death was, then, also the liberator to the new and true life of the
spirit freed of the crippling results of the fall. The horror film
teaches an acceptance of the natural order of things and an affirma-
tion of man's ability to cope with and even prevail over the evil of life
which he can never hope to understand; death is the unknown and
unknowable end to life, but it is also the natural and peaceful end
to the turmoil and terror of life in a fallen world. To die in irre-
deemable sin is the primary danger in the morality play; to be unable to die and find peace and the possibility of heaven for the suffering spirit is the great danger in the horror film.

I have certainly set the horror film a mighty task—to make us accept death as the natural ending of life, an ending to be desired.
But that task is really no more possible or impossible than any of the
tasks art ever attempts. The bold method of the horror film is as old
as Aristotle and older; it sets out to purge us of our fear of death by
exposing us to death as we have never seen it before, by distorting
the fact of death into all possible contortions to help us see its simple and natural reality. The mirror the horror film holds up to death
is the distorting mirror of a deserted funhouse which frightens us
out of fear and frees our fancy to find the truth more surely.

Death in the horror film is most often grotesque; innocent and
guilty alike are slaughtered horribly—drained of their blood by
vampires, strangled or flung aside casually by a mummy's hand or
the sewn hand of a monster made from dead flesh and bone, mangled by a werewolf's teeth and claws, strangled by the severed hands
of a dead man, given to savage and unnatural beasts by mad and
sadistic scientists, burked by a body snatcher desperate for a fresh
corpse, and on and hideously on. But what is more horrible, even
death and the repose of the grave are impermanent; the dead rise
or are disturbed in a variety of ways: they rise as vampires thirsting
for blood, their mummified remains return after nearly four thousand years to seek revenge for the desecration of a princess' tomb,

they are eaten by ghouls and snatched by body snatchers, their bodies are dissected and sewn together anew as a monster, they are enslaved as zombies, and, if nothing worse, they are dug up for inspection by those left fighting whatever evil killed them.

The central figure of the film, the monster of evil whatever his particular form, suffers perhaps worst of all from the failure of death, and his grotesque death not only saves the world he inhabits from his evil, but also frees him into a natural and permanent death from the painful striving of his unnatural life. The vampire is peaceful and his features calm and even beautiful once the stake is driven through his heart, his head severed, and his mouth stuffed with garlic; the Frankenstein monster's blundering search for understanding and love in a society which is horrified by him is at the only end it could possibly have; the mummy's centuries of living death are resolved in a true death; the madman is freed of his distorting insanity; the invisible man, whose invisibility imprisoned his mind as it freed his flesh, rests quietly and visibly. This peace, the peace of death, is the object and end of the horror film; it is not merely the peace which follows the destruction of an antagonist, for it benefits the villainous opponent as well as his heroic slayers.

The werewolf story is perhaps the clearest example of this important ambiguity of death in the horror film. The werewolf, whether one considers *The Werewolf of London* or *The Wolf Man* or any of their long line of imitators, is the hero as well as the villain of the film. He is an innocent man who has been bitten by a werewolf and has, because of the supernatural properties of the bite, become a werewolf himself, doomed to change under the full moon into a wolf who must kill to stay alive. Through no action of his own the evil and madness inherent in every fallen man is released in him, or, as the gypsy's poem in *The Wolf Man* has it:

> Even a man who is pure at heart
>   And says his prayers by night
> May become a wolf when the wolfbane blooms
>   And the moon is full and bright.

He destroys life and hurts the one he loves, but he cannot stop himself. As a wolf, he is a creature of blind animal evil; as a man, he suffers the tortures of the damned, for he knows the evil he does and can do nothing about it. Walking through a normal environment in a business suit, he is separated only by the anguish of his face from the ordinary pattern of natural life, a life made intensely beautiful in its mundanity by his separation from it and by the alienation of his darker self from all of its standards, its humanity, its simple decencies. He can only die, as the best version of the story has it, by a wound from a silver weapon (a knife, a bullet, the head of a cane) wielded by one who loves him dearly.

This situation makes great demands of the observer, the theater-goer in his plush seat, for he must wish for the hero's victory, his release from the curse, by desiring that he die, that he be killed by someone who loves him. Death itself, our final villain, must be made the instrument of the hero's salvation. This is a paradox worthy of the highest art, for here the spiritual struggle of one man bursts out into the visible world in hair, claws, and fangs, and the cruelty of man's love for his fellows is painfully enacted in the murder of love, the sacrifice for the last victory of the soul. When Lawrence Talbot lies in the arms of his father, his evil pelt gone in death, he is no Oedipus nor poisoned Hamlet, but his story is akin to theirs—he is the victim of the nature of a fallen world, and his death restores what order there is possible to that world. The act of love that killed him was one of overwhelming sacrifice, and its victory is para-doxical and incomprehensible to the reason of our normal world. The werewolf film is a work of fantasy and thus, to eyes and minds trained by realistic standards, it seems a fragile and finally insignifi-cant entertainment. But, whatever the merits of its performance, its form and lines are sound. Its revelation of the dark and its affirma-tion of redeeming love are valid; its metaphysics and its moral struc-ture, whatever their variance from theological standards, are true to the Christian understanding and perhaps even, for those of you who demand it, to a modern existential understanding of the quality of our lives, of the way things really are.

The other central figures in the best horror films, the ones which have become a part of all our memories, are also victims as well as villains: vampires who are undead by no choice of their own, mon-sters who are placed in a world that doesn't want them and hates them, mummies who are driven by a curse put on them by long-dead priests of a religion which is also dead. All of these creatures find the victory of peace in the defeat of death. And we are, then, doubly re-lieved at their deaths and perhaps saddened, too. In this ambiguity the beauty lies, the poetry inextricably a part of the danger.

But what of the living, those who survive the horrors and live on at the end of the film? I said that the horror film (as, I suspect, all great art must) affirms man's ability to cope with evil beyond his ken and even to prevail over it. The elements of that enduring ability are two, a working combination of reason and faith, of practical understanding and belief. Neither is properly efficacious without the other. Belief alone may save one's soul, but it will give him only the direction for any temporal and practical victory. The priest and the superstitious gypsy are allied in belief, for they both know that there are things in this world beyond the scope of reason and of scientific thought. Their knowledge is ineffectual however, because it is too often fatalistic; they hold the devil in too high regard to strive to foil him; they will pray for the dead, but they can offer little beyond spiritual solace to the living. Reason, too, is ineffectual, because it denies the existence of any evil that does not fit the immutable laws of a logical and orderly universe. The myriad doctors, scientists, and believers in a rational world are baffled by occurrences which can fit in no possible way into their system; they examine the happenings of the night by daylight and cannot understand the mysteries of the dark. Theirs is a more foolish innocence than that of the superstitious peasant, for their scientific optimism often leads them to deny evil as an active force in human affairs altogether.

Evil must be known to be combated, and the knowing must lead to respect for its power but never to fearful surrender to it. He who can fuse reason and belief into an imaginative and active force is the hero of the horror film, but he is neither the tragic hero nor the comic hero. He is not even the central figure of the story, for although he restores order by his action, he does not control the movement of events at all (no Hamlet is he, nor powerful Prospero). Rather he copes with events beyond human control. He is the older and wiser guide who reveals the mystery to the votary. The usual pattern is that a young, intelligent person is suddenly faced with an evil beyond his grasp, an evil which does not usually shatter his will to resist but which does leave him stripped of illusions and unable to defend himself properly. An older man (a former teacher, a professor interested in the occult, a scientist, even on occasion a priest) arrives and teaches the young man to respect all truth no matter what its sources and to fight with what weapons are needed, whether they be the practical weapons of violent force or the incantations and rituals of primitive belief.

Edward Van Sloan is the actor who always seemed to be this heroic guide, perhaps because as Professor Abraham Van Helsing in *Dracula* he surely rendered most fully the strength of this figure—brave, intelligent, aware of the limitations of his humanity, but never faltering in his quest for securing the safety of those menaced by evil, for restoring order. He is a fully educated and practical man with an understanding of modern science and philosophy, but he never rejects the wisdom and beliefs of older orders and systems, whether they be the Transylvanian lore of vampires and werewolves, the curses of the ancient Egyptians (Van Sloan as Dr. Muller in *The Mummy*, 1932), or the old belief that there are directions in which man must not inquire and search too far without breaking the bounds set for him by God (again Van Sloan as Dr. Waldman in *Frankenstein*). He prevails over the personifications of evil, not because he is superior to it in power and appeal, but rather because he is human, weak, and fallen but continually striving to better himself and his world, to earn some of the love which is his by God's grace.

This heroic man and the young people whom he guides fight for human values and the natural order of things, the right to live freely without submitting to evil and the right to die peacefully and forever. The evil they do battle with, for all its supernatural trappings, is also human—the vampires and werewolves, monsters and mummies are all human at source and are all personifications of that potentiality for evil and sin which is so much a part of us all. Hero and villain are much the same—both human, both flawed unto death—and the complexity of their struggle and the dark nature of the order recovered by that struggle give the horror film its moral and metaphysical weight. It is a morality play for our times, approaching the very paradox of human life in its fantastic simplicity. It is religious and as mysterious as all art finally proves to be; it transmutes danger into poetry and affirms humanity in the very face of horror.

GOTHIC HORROR

Two Archetypes: The Frankenstein Monster and the Vampire

Brides of Dracula

BRAM STOKER

❖◆◆◆◆◆◆◆◆◆◆◆◆◆◆◆◆◆◆◆◆◆◆◆◆◆◆◆◆◆◆◆◆◆◆◆◆◆❖

JONATHAN HARKER'S JOURNAL

Later: the morning of 16 May.—God preserve my sanity, for to this I am reduced. Safety and the assurance of safety are things of the past. Whilst I live on here there is but one thing to hope for, that I may not go mad, if, indeed, I be not mad already. If I be sane, then surely it is maddening to think that of all the foul things that lurk in this hateful place the Count is the least dreadful to me; that to him alone I can look for safety, even though this be only whilst I can serve his purpose. Great God! merciful God. Let me be calm, for out of that way lies madness indeed. I begin to get new lights on certain things which have puzzled me. Up to now I never quite knew what Shakespeare meant when he made Hamlet say:—

> "My tablets! quick, my tablets!
> 'Tis meet that I put it down," etc.,

From the novel Dracula *by Bram Stoker. First published in England in 1897.*

for now, feeling as though my own brain were unhinged or as if the shock had come which must end in its undoing, I turn to my diary for repose. The habit of entering accurately must help to soothe me.

The Count's mysterious warning [not to fall asleep in another part of the castle] frightened me at the time; it frightens me more now when I think of it, for in the future he has a fearful hold upon me. I shall fear to doubt what he may say!

When I had written in my diary and had fortunately replaced the book and pen in my pocket I felt sleepy. The Count's warning came into my mind, but I took a pleasure in disobeying it. The sense of sleep was upon me, and with it the obstinacy which sleep brings as outrider. The soft moonlight soothed, and the wide expanse without gave a sense of freedom which refreshed me. I determined not to return to-night to the gloom-haunted rooms, but to sleep here, where, of old, ladies had sat and sung and lived sweet lives whilst their gentle breasts were sad for their menfolk away in the midst of remorseless wars. I drew a great couch out of its place near the corner, so that as I lay, I could look at the lovely view to east and south, and unthinking of and uncaring for the dust, composed myself for sleep. I suppose I must have fallen asleep; I hope so, but I fear, for all that followed was startlingly real—so real that now sitting here in the broad, full sunlight of the morning, I cannot in the least believe that it was all sleep.

I was not alone. The room was the same, unchanged in any way since I came into it; I could see along the floor, in the brilliant moonlight, my own footsteps marked where I had disturbed the long accumulation of dust. In the moonlight opposite me were three young women, ladies by their dress and manner. I thought at the time that I must be dreaming when I saw them, for, though the moonlight was behind them, they threw no shadow on the floor. They came close to me, and looked at me for some time, and then whispered together. Two were dark, and had high aquiline noses, like the Count, and great dark, piercing eyes, that seemed to be almost red when contrasted with the pale yellow moon. The other was fair, as fair as can be, with great wavy masses of golden hair and eyes like pale sapphires. I seemed somehow to know her face, and to know it in connection with some dreamy fear, but I could not recollect at the moment how or where. All three had brilliant white teeth that shone like pearls against the ruby of their voluptuous lips. There was something about them that made me uneasy, some longing and at the same time some deadly fear. I felt in my heart a wicked, burn-

ing desire that they would kiss me with those red lips. It is not good
to note this down, lest some day it should meet Mina's eyes and cause
her pain; but it is the truth. They whispered together, and then they
all three laughed—such a silvery, musical laugh, but as hard as
though the sound never could have come through the softness of
human lips. It was like the intolerable, tingling sweetness of water-
glasses when played on by a cunning hand. The fair girl shook her
head coquettishly, and the other two urged her on. One said:—

"Go on! You are first, and we shall follow; yours is the right to
begin." The other added:—

"He is young and strong; there are kisses for us all." I lay
quiet, looking out under my eyelashes in an agony of delightful anticipation. The fair girl advanced and bent over me till I could feel
the movement of her breath upon me. Sweet it was in one sense,
honey sweet, and sent the same tingling through the nerves as her
voice, but with a bitter underlying the sweet, a bitter offensiveness,
as one smells in blood.

I was afraid to raise my eyelids, but looked out and saw perfectly
under the lashes. The girl went on her knees, and bent over me, simply gloating. There was a deliberate voluptuousness which was both
thrilling and repulsive, and as she arched her neck she actually licked
her lips like an animal, till I could see in the moonlight the mois-
ture shining on the scarlet lips and on the red tongue as it lapped
the white sharp teeth. Lower and lower went her head as the lips
went below the range of my mouth and chin and seemed to fasten
on my throat. Then she paused, and I could hear the churning
sound of her tongue as it licked her teeth and lips, and I could feel
the hot breath on my neck. Then the skin on my throat began to
tingle as one's flesh does when the hand that is to tickle it approaches
nearer—nearer. I could feel the soft, shivering touch of the lips on
the super-sensitive skin of my throat, and the hard dents of two
sharp teeth, just touching and pausing there. I closed my eyes in a
languorous ecstasy and waited—and waited with beating heart.

But at that instant, another sensation swept through me as quick
as lightning. I was conscious of the presence of the Count, and of his
being as if lapped in a storm of fury. As my eyes opened involun-
tarily I saw his strong hand grasp the slender neck of the fair woman
and with giant's power draw it back, the blue eyes transformed with
fury, the white teeth champing with rage, and the fair cheeks blazing
red with passion. But the Count! Never did I imagine such wrath
and fury, even to the demons of the pit. His eyes were positively

blazing. The red light in them was lurid, as if the flames of hell-fire blazed behind them. His face was deathly pale, and the lines of it were hard like drawn wires; the thick eyebrows that met over the nose now seemed like a heaving bar of white-hot metal. With a fierce sweep of his arm, he hurled the woman from him, and then motioned to the others, as though he were beating them back; it was the same imperious gesture that I had seen used to the wolves. In a voice which, though low and almost in a whisper seemed to cut through the air and then ring round the room he said:—

"How dare you touch him, any of you? How dare you cast eyes on him when I had forbidden it? Back, I tell you all! This man belongs to me! Beware how you meddle with him, or you'll have to deal with me." The fair girl, with a laugh of ribald coquetry, turned to answer him:—

"You yourself never loved; you never love!" On this the other women joined, and such a mirthless, hard, soulless laughter rang through the room that it almost made me faint to hear; it seemed like the pleasure of fiends. Then the Count turned, after looking at my face attentively, and said in a soft whisper:—

"Yes, I too can love; you yourselves can tell it from the past. Is it not so? Well, now I promise you that when I am done with him you shall kiss him at your will. Now go! go! I must awaken him, for there is work to be done."

"Are we to have nothing to-night?" said one of them, with a low laugh, as she pointed to the bag which he had thrown upon the floor, and which moved as though there were some living thing within it. For answer he nodded his head. One of the women jumped forward and opened it. If my ears did not deceive me there was a gasp and a low wail, as of a half-smothered child. The women closed round, whilst I was aghast with horror; but as I looked they disappeared, and with them the dreadful bag. There was no door near them, and they could not have passed me without my noticing. They simply seemed to fade into the rays of the moonlight and pass out through the window, for I could see outside the dim, shadowy forms for a moment before they entirely faded away.

Then the horror overcame me, and I sank down unconscious. . . .

DR. VAN HELSING'S MEMORANDUM

5 November, afternoon.—I am at least sane. Thank God for that mercy at all events, though the proving it has been dreadful. When

I left Madam Mina sleeping within the Holy circle, I took my way to the castle. The blacksmith hammer which I took in the carriage from Veresti was useful; though the doors were all open I broke them off the rusty hinges, lest some ill-intent or ill-chance should close them, so that being entered I might not get out. Jonathan's bitter experience served me here. By memory of his diary I found my way to the old chapel, for I knew that here my work lay. The air was oppressive; it seemed as if there was some sulphurous fume, which at times made me dizzy. Either there was a roaring in my ears or I heard afar off the howl of wolves. Then I bethought me of my dear Madam Mina, and I was in terrible plight. The dilemma had me between his horns.

Her, I had not dare to take into this place, but left safe from the Vampire in that Holy circle; and yet even there would be the wolf! I resolve me that my work lay here, and that as to the wolves we must submit, if it were God's will. At any rate it was only death and freedom beyond. So did I choose for her. Had it but been for myself the choice had been easy, the maw of the wolf were better to rest in than the grave of the Vampire! So I make my choice to go on with my work.

I knew that there were at least three graves to find—graves that are inhabit; so I search, and search, and I find one of them. She lay in her Vampire sleep, so full of life and voluptuous beauty that I shudder as though I have come to do murder. Ah, I doubt not that in the old time, when such things were, many a man who set forth to do such a task as mine, found at the last his heart fail him, and then his nerve. So he delay, and delay, and delay, till the mere beauty and the fascination of the wanton Un-Dead have hypnotise him; and he remain on and on, till sunset come, and the Vampire sleep be over. Then the beautiful eyes of the fair woman open and look love, and the voluptuous mouth present to a kiss—and man is weak. And there remain one more victim in the Vampire fold; one more to swell the grim and grisly ranks of the Un-Dead! . . .

There is some fascination, surely, when I am moved by the mere presence of such a one, even lying as she lay in a tomb fretted with age and heavy with the dust of centuries, though there be that hor-rid odour such as the lairs of the Count have had. Yes, I was moved —I, Van Helsing, with all my purpose and with my motive for hate —I was moved to a yearning for delay which seemed to paralyse my faculties and to clog my very soul. It may have been that the need of natural sleep, and the strange oppression of the air were beginning to overcome me. Certain it was that I was lapsing into sleep, the open-eyed sleep of one who yields to a sweet fascination, when there came through the snow-stilled air a long, low wail, so full of woe and pity that it woke me like the sound of a clarion. For it was the voice of my dear Madam Mina that I heard.

Then I braced myself again to my horrid task, and found by wrenching away tomb-tops one other of the sisters, the other dark one. I dared not pause to look on her as I had on her sister, lest once more I should begin to be enthrall; but I go on searching until, presently, I find in a high great tomb as if made to one much beloved that other fair sister which, like Jonathan I had seen to gather herself out of the atoms of the mist. She was so fair to look on, so radiantly beautiful, so exquisitely voluptuous, that the very instinct of man in me, which calls some of my sex to love and to protect one of hers, made my head whirl with new emotion. But God be thanked, that soul-wail of my dear Madam Mina had not died out of my ears; and, before the spell could be wrought further upon me, I had nerved myself to my wild work. By this time I had searched all the tombs in the chapel, so far as I could tell; and as there had been only three of these Un-Dead phantoms around us in the night, I took it that there were no more of active Un-Dead existent. There was one great tomb more lordly than all the rest; huge it was, and nobly proportioned. On it was but one word

DRACULA

This then was the Un-Dead home of the King-Vampire, to whom so many more were due. Its emptiness spoke eloquent to make certain what I knew. Before I began to restore these women to their dead selves through my awful work, I laid in Dracula's tomb some of the Wafer, and so banished him from it, Un-Dead, for ever.

Then began my terrible task, and I dreaded it. Had it been but one, it had been easy, comparative. But three! To begin twice more after I had been through a deed of horror; for it was terrible with the sweet Miss Lucy, what would it not be with these strange ones who had survived through centuries, and who had been strengthened by the passing of the years; who would, if they could, have fought for their foul lives. . . .

Oh, my friend John, but it was butcher work; had I not been nerved by thoughts of other dead, and of the living over whom hung such a pall of fear, I could not have gone on. I tremble and tremble even yet, though till all was over, God be thanked, my nerve did stand. Had I not seen the repose in the first place, and the gladness that stole over it just ere the final dissolution came, as realisation that the soul had been won, I could not have gone further with my butchery. I could not have endured the horrid screeching as the stake drove home; the plunging of writhing form, and lips of bloody foam. I should have fled in terror and left my work undone. But it is over! And the poor souls, I can pity them now and weep, as I think of them placid each in her full sleep of death for a short moment ere fading. For, friend John, hardly had my knife severed the head of each, before the whole body began to melt away and crumble into its native dust, as though the death that should have come centuries agone had at last assert himself and say at once and loud "I am here!"

Before I left the castle I so fixed its entrances that never more can the Count enter there Un-Dead.

When I stepped into the circle where Madam Mina slept, she woke from her sleep and, seeing me, cried out in pain that I had endured too much.

"Come!" she said, "come away from this awful place! Let us go to meet my husband who is, I know, coming towards us." She was looking thin and pale and weak; but her eyes were pure and glowed with fervour. I was glad to see her paleness and her illness, for my mind was full of the fresh horror of that ruddy vampire sleep.

And so with trust and hope, and yet full of fear, we go eastward to meet our friends—and *him*—whom Madam Mina tell me that she *know* are coming to meet us.

Vampire's Progress: *Dracula* from Novel to Film via Broadway

ROY HUSS

❖◆◆◆❖

Tod Browning's *Dracula* is a film of missed opportunities, a piece of work that is shackled by the producer's decision to capitalize upon the success of Balderston and Deane's stage adaptation of Bram Stoker's classic novel rather than to exploit the greater cinematic suggestiveness of the novel itself. Although there have of course been truly filmic screen adaptations of plays, Browning seemed inclined to accept the exigencies of the stage in shaping this film. In the resulting "photoplay" he seems to regard the frame of his camera's viewfinder merely as a proscenium arch to be filled in with performers and background decor, hardly ever as a creative instrument which might wrench from his material—by changing the angle and perspective of the camera—the essence of the more dynamic and dramatic relationships between characters and objects. When the camera moves, it is merely to pursue, like a spotlight, the movements of the actors, not to "create" the special cinematic continuum of space and time in which "reality" could be heightened.

The few exceptions to this static staginess are nevertheless memorable. In a sequence at Dr. Seward's sanitarium, a shot in which Dracula's face, shown in close-up, slides down off the lower left-hand corner of the frame as he bites Mina's neck for the first time is striking. This shot is paralleled later by a close-up of Mina's immobile, trancelike face moving off-frame in the same manner, as her growing vampirism prompts a blood-lust movement toward her fiancé. One has to admit, however, that these two moments of cinematic effectiveness may have been inspired simply by Browning's desire to keep a gruesome sight off-screen.

For the most part it is only when Browning seeks to expand the action beyond the walls of Dr. Seward's sanitarium—where the entire action of the play and the major part of the film is set—and so goes directly back to Stoker's Gothic masterpiece for his material, that we are given any real hints of what Browning is capable of as a filmmaker. In an opening sequence in the film, for instance—the one depicting the lawyer Renfield's journey by carriage to Castle Dracula —Browning is forced to evolve some cinematic artistry to cope with the swift and horrendous motion of the carriage in its midnight passage through the Carpathian mountains. Out of this he admirably composes a montage of shots to invoke a sense of speed and terror:

(1) high-angle panoramic sightings of the vulnerably small black vehicle being dragged at breakneck pace through the desolate countryside, intercut with (2) shots of the bouncing interior of the coach showing Renfield's discomfort, followed by a cut to (3) a medium shot of the bat, into which the driver (Dracula himself) has been transformed, controlling the horses by flying over

their heads; then a cut to (4) a medium reaction shot of Renfield leaning out of the carriage to chastise the driver and finding the driver's seat empty; and ending with a cut to (5) the driverless carriage suddenly coming to a rattling halt in the sombre blackness of the castle's courtyard.

This is exactly the kind of composition of episodes that one discovers in Stoker's novel, in which normal space-time continuums are constantly restructured in a filmic way for dramatic effect. (It is good to keep in mind that Griffith was influenced by Dickens, not by the theater.) In Stoker's tale, however, the carriage ride is different in certain particulars: the mysterious driver (here, also, Dracula himself) stops the coach many times en route in order to pursue by foot a strange blue flame which appears deep within the forest. (We later learn that on Walpurgis Nacht, blue lights appear over spots where treasure is buried, and thus we discover an unsuspected monetary interest in Dracula's character. After all, the undead, like every one else, must live!) There is in the incident no metamorphosis in Dracula's form, but he is able to ward off with a simple ritualistic gesture a circle of wolves that are all the more menacing because of their initial silence. (Compare this with the noiseless stares of the wolves in the dream of Freud's famous "wolf-man" patient).

The arrival of the ship bearing Dracula lying in suspended animation in his box of Transylvanian soil was another episode in the novel upon which Browning had to rely in order to piece out the play. Strangely enough neither the novel nor the film reveals details of the voyage itself. Certainly it must have been the most macabre sailing since that of the Ancient Mariner, for we are told later (in the novel) that it was Dracula who had devised the storm and the uncanny mist following it as a cover for his landing. And since we are also told of Dracula's blood-thirst for London's "teeming millions," it is not hard to imagine the grisly fate of the ship's crew.

But in Browning's use of these scenes we also find a marked departure from the novel. Whereas Stoker allows us to see, from the shore through Mina's eyes, the strange course of the unmanned ship —a vignette in which impressions of a storm at sea are unsurpassed by fictional realism—Browning gives us a rather short-hand, highly stylized rendition: a couple of tight shots of an unreal-looking, full-rigged set of masts above an obscure hulk bobbing in wind and wave.

In the film the scene that immediately follows the storm sequence is equally stagey, but this time influenced more by the viable German expressionistic theater, from which directors such as Lang, Murnau, and Wiene drew some of their cinematic vitality, than by the flat naturalism of the Broadway production. With the dramatic shot of merely the shadow of the dead captain strapped to the helm, magnified as it is projected on a wall, we have another inkling of what this film might have been. For as horror classics such as *Diabolique* have shown, two of the most effective ingredients of the genre are suggestibility and distortion. The brief shadow-on-the-wall episode in Browning's film has both: by suggesting rather than portraying the victimized corpse of the captain, the director leaves the imagination of the audience free to create a more personal sense of grotesquerie;[1] and by distorting the image in projection and magnification as a shadow, he puts us under the same spell woven by theatrical expressionism, giving us a feeling that reality is shaped by the mental images projected upon it, that life may after all be a dream—or a nightmare! [2]

Needless to say there is no representation of the ship and the storm in Balderston and Deane's stage adaptation of *Dracula*. In lieu of even a passing reference to the mysterious voyage, the adaptors supply a quaint explanation of how Dracula got to England, one that clearly identifies the play's vintage as 1927, the year of Lindbergh's historic transatlantic flight. Van Helsing surmises that Dracula, together with his crates of earth, must have been transported to England by chartered plane, for, he argues, this is the only way of reaching London from Transylvania between sunset and sunrise, the period of a vampire's potency.

The stage version of *Dracula* is of course not without its fascination. Bold theatricality in the use of props no doubt accounted in large part for its resounding success. The mechanical bat which, suspended from a wire, is flown in from the terrace; the movements of the empty swivel chair indicating Dracula's invisible presence in the room; the secret panel that allows Dracula to enter unobserved so

---

[1] Another example of such suggestiveness—this time found in the novel but not in the film—occurs when Dracula, in order to compensate his wives for denying them Harker for their blood banquet, offers a bag containing the outlines of some moving creature. Our imaginations are left to ponder the contents of the "dreadful bag."

[2] In *Nosferatu*, the 1922 version of the vampire story by Murnau, this kind of German theatrical expressionism is brilliantly used in a scene in which the vampire's hands and body are shown as an elongated shadow on the wall as he approaches his victim.

that his head or hand can emerge from behind the sofa bathed in an eerie green light—all these must have produced electrifying effects. But the techniques themselves are of course strictly *du theatre*, never cinematic.

Be that as it may, the stage version of *Dracula* provides an interesting perspective from which to contrast the film and the novel. The authors of the play naturally sought to make the novel's plot more stringent and the relationships between the characters more closeknit. Dr. Seward, merely a friend and devotee of the victimized Mina in the novel, becomes her father both in the play and in the film. Mina's fiancé, Jonathan Harker, the terrorized guest at Castle Dracula in Stoker's novel, is replaced in Browning's film by Renfield, whose madness, induced by the vampire's sting, fills him with a voracious appetite for flies and spiders. In both the novel and the play Renfield's insanity is a *donnée*—he has been an inveterate mental patient at Dr. Seward's sanitarium. But Browning uses Renfield's horrendous experiences at Castle Dracula to explain the focus of his strange obsession: upon his arrival there the lawyer suffers the minor trauma of having to push his way through a huge web on which a large spider lunges after a trapped fly. In the play Renfield's locus in the plot is little more than that of a convenient piece of stage machinery: his fits and sudden appearances are devices for getting characters out of the way so that Dracula may make his sinister entrances unobserved by the others. In the novel the insane Renfield is used not only to provide a macabre atmosphere but also to illustrate the existential plight of being dehumanized as both villain and victim (for it is he who first invites Dracula to enter the house before being mangled by him). Stoker also hints that he is a Dracula *manqué,* a defective product of the same conjunction of elemental forces that spawned the master.

The character and personality of Jonathan Harker suffer an unfortunate loss of dimension in both play and film. Whereas in the novel Jonathan has admirable fortitude and endurance as Dracula's victim, and later great heroic verve and dash as his vanquisher, his role on the stage and in the film is merely that of the simpering, lovestruck young man.

The horror film genre seems to reserve no place for the dashing young hero-savior. In science fiction films his mental as well physical strength is needed to defeat the extra-terrestrial monster (or other menace) after the death or mental breakdown of the old scientist in charge, and his reward is that at the end he gets the heroine (usually the old scientist's daughter, perhaps herself a scientist or lab technician). But in the more classic horror film his function in the plot is to act as an instrument for the older, wiser priest-magician-exorciser. The "Oedipal" victory of the *juvenis* over the *senex* for the favors of the maiden that Northrop Frye finds to be the pattern in comedy is here, in the horror film, ironically reversed. Not that the authority-father figure gets or even wants the young girl; but it is his mentality representing the wisdom of the past rather than the instinctual vigor of youth that is triumphant.

Both the play version and the film version of *Dracula* are "true to genre" in that it is Van Helsing's stamina that wins the day—it is he who seeks out Dracula in his tomb and drives the stake through his heart. When we turn back to Stoker's novel, however, we find this generic stereotype to be violated. Here we are surprised to discover that Van Helsing's energies fail him in the end. Even though it is his knowledge and initiative that have brought both Dracula's true identity and the means of combatting him to light, he reverts to the old man's role of an ancient priest guarding Mina, now a kind of oracle-goddess in telepathic contact with Dracula's mind. He must also perform the less taxing old man's work of destroying the immobile bodies of Dracula's wives and sanctifying their tombs, but it remains for the young—particularly Jonathan and the impulsive American—to dispatch Dracula and his gypsy bodyguards with sword and knife in traditional derring-do adventure-romance fashion rather than with the wooden stake of prescribed priestly ritual.

In the film the character Mina, Jonathan's fiancée and later his wife, also suffers a loss of complexity and function. Stoker conceives of her as having a feminine tenderness and intuition blended to such a remarkable degree with what Van Helsing calls a "masculine intelligence" and persistence that she gradually moves into the role of "tribal goddess" among her male devotees. It is she who most directly brings about Dracula's ruin. Both Browning and the stage adaptors, however, cast her into the traditional Victorian role of heroine in distress. Here neither her male toughness of mind nor her female intuition is instrumental in Dracula's defeat. For Browning and the stage adaptors she is merely a sentimental Dickensian heroine; for Stoker she is more of a George Eliot one.

The female principle found in the novel is seriously watered down in another way in the film. In the novel the counterpart for Mina's delicate balance of sensibility and reason is found in the wily seductiveness of Dracula's wives. Since the Transylvanian episodes would have taxed dramatic unity, these characters have no part in the play. In the film we are introduced to them in a brief interlude inserted into the sequence showing Renfield's carriage journey to the castle. We see them emerging, along with Dracula, from their coffins in the rat-infested dungeon in order to prepare for the arrival of their lawyer guest. The only other time we see them is during an effective but all too brief scene in which Renfield, having fallen to the floor, is approached by the three figures trailing their white gowns as zombielike they move toward him in their blood-thirst.[3]

Abandoned as they are in this scene by the director, the wives of Dracula certainly constitute a loose end in the plot of the film. Does Dracula take them with him to England? If so, does Van Helsing stay behind in the crypt at Carfax Abbey in order to destroy them? If they remained in Transylvania (as shown in the novel), wouldn't they continue to be a menace, thus implicitly marring the film's happy ending? Stoker's reintroduction of them later in the action of course solves these problems for the novel: after their abortive attempt upon Jonathan, and, near the end, their temptation of Mina (who is by now their near sister in vampirism), we witness the gruesome spectacle of the death of these undead.

But Browning's abbreviation of the role of Dracula's wives causes not only a disfigurement of the plot. As I have already hinted, the film almost obliterates the thematic import of their characterizations, diluting Stoker's more circumspect view of what is quintessentially feminine. In the novel Mina's Victorian passivity, romanticism, and helplessness are transformed under duress into what is most viable in the female— a strong intuition tempered by a certain intellectual initiative and manual dexterity (demonstrated, for example, by her collation of all the diaries and journals). As a contrast Stoker redeploys the wives in order to display what the Victorian mind would regard as an antivalue: the seemingly oversexed enchantress, the *femme fatale,* in fact the "vamp" (from *vampire*), as she came to be called later on. Dracula's wives are all the more loathesome because their almost irresistible sexual appeal masks a lust that is more primitive: a sexual fantasy of oral incorporation that is grotesque to see so blatantly acted out because it is a repressed part of our own being. Although never exploited by Browning, the three episodes in the novel dealing with Dracula's wives have be-

[3] Browning's clumsy attempt to "telegraph" this scene by having the innkeeper's wife warn Renfield that Dracula lives in the castle with three women who suck blood seems utterly superfluous.

come a fountainhead for scenes in later horror films featuring the vampire as *femme fatale*—the type of role in which Barbara Steele specializes.

Insofar as Browning's *Dracula* retains any life, it is probably due to its quaintness as "camp"—how many of us have patiently sat and waited to savor once again Lugosi's "Children of the Night" speech? But scarcely can we be held by this movie's all too sporadic display of filmic effects. If we go back to it after saturating ourselves with Bram Stoker's masterpiece, we can not help but regard the story's progress from novel to screen via Broadway as a patent example of artistic retrogression.

On the Nightmare of Bloodsucking
ERNEST JONES

◆◆◆

. . . As to the essential attribute of the Vampire, namely *Bloodsucking,* we find a great many predecessors of the Vampire proper. In general it may be said that the habit of sucking living blood is throughout connected with ideas of cannibalism on the one hand and the Incubat-Succubat,[1] two facts which alone reveal the sexual origin of the belief. The Assyrian and Babylonian Lilats, the Eastern Palukah, the Finnish Lord of the Underworld, the Bohemian Mora, the German Alp: all suck human blood. The Ludak of the Laplanders appears in the form of a bug and sucks blood through an iron tube. The Malayan Molong, as well as the Penangelam of Indo-China, visit women at night and live on the human blood they suck.

From On the Nightmare *by Ernest Jones (New York: Liveright Publishing Corp., 1971), pp. 116–25. Copyright © 1951, 1971 by Liveright Publishing Corporation. Reprinted by permission of Liveright Publishing Corp., the Hogarth Press, and Mrs. Katharine Jones.*

[1] Incubi and Succubi were demons who descended upon their victims during sleep and forced them to have sexual intercourse. The former attacked women; the latter, men. The victims remained sleeping, but had nightmares [Editors' note].

The sexual nature of the act is plainly indicated in the following examples. Heinrich von Wlislocki, in his researches into Roumanian superstitions, tells us: "The Nosferat not only sucks the blood of sleeping people, but also does mischief as an Incubus or Succubus. The Nosferat is the still-born, illegitimate child of two people who are similarly illegitimate. It is hardly put under the earth before it awakes to life and leaves its grave never to return. It visits people by night in the form of a black cat, a black dog, a beetle, a butterfly or even a simple straw. When its sex is male, it visits women; when female, men. With young people it indulges in sexual orgies until they get ill and die of exhaustion. In this case it also appears in the form of a handsome youth or a pretty girl, while the victim lies half awake and submits unresistingly. It often happens that women are impregnated by the creature and bear children who can be recognized by their ugliness and by their having hair over the whole body. They then always become witches, usually Moroiu.[2] The Nosferat appears to bridegrooms and brides and makes them impotent and sterile." The Chaldeans believed in the existence of spirits who had intercourse with mortals in their sleep, devoured their flesh and sucked their blood; a complete Jack the Ripper phantasy. The Vedic Gandharvas are bloodthirsty lewd demons who visit women in their sleep. Similar to them are the Indian Pisâchas, who lust after flesh and indulge their cruel pleasure on women when these are asleep, drunk or insane. Other beings of the same kind devote their attention rather to men; thus the Ruthenian Upierzyca when the moon is full seeks youths in their bed and consumes them in kisses and embraces. Freimark writes: "The Greek and Roman Lamias are at the same time lewd demons and Vampires. They try to get handsome strong youths to fall in love with them and to marry them. Having succeeded in this, they kill them by sucking their blood." Finally, one may remark that the present-day use of the word, particularly current since the War, speaks in the same direction: a film Vampire is a beautiful woman who uses her sexual charms for anal-sadistic purposes.

Blood is not the only vital fluid extracted from the victim, though the Vampire proper generally confines himself to it. The German *Alp* sucks the nipples of men and children, and withdraws milk from

---

[2] Elsewhere Jones points out that in Greek Orthodoxy "children born on Christmas day are doomed to become vampires in punishment for their mother's sin of being so presumptuous as to conceive on the same day as the Virgin Mary." Under the Roman Church, however, these same children were suspected of being werewolves. Hammer Films explores this latter motif in *Curse of the Werewolf* (1961), directed by Terence Fisher [Editors' note].

women and cows more often than blood. The Drud also sucks the breasts of children, while the Southern Slav Mora sucks blood or milk indifferently. In India, the Churel, after spending a night with a handsome young man sucks his very "life" out.

The explanation of these phantasies is surely not hard. A nightly visit from a beautiful or frightful being, who first exhausts the sleeper with passionate embraces and then withdraws from him a vital fluid: all this can point only to a natural and common process, namely to nocturnal emissions accompanied with dreams of a more or less erotic nature. In the unconscious mind blood is commonly an equivalent for semen, and it is not necessary to have recourse, as Hock does, to the possibility of "wounds inflicted on oneself by scratching during a voluptuous dream."

Many myths and legends afford strongly confirmatory evidence of this conclusion. To begin with, the Accadian Gelal and Kiel Galal, the Assyrian Sil and Sileth, who are equivalent to the European Incubus and Succubus, are demons whose special function it was to bring about nocturnal emissions by nocturnal embraces. According to Quedenfeldt, south of the Atlas mountains there prevails the belief that there are old negresses who at night suck blood from the *toes* of those asleep. The Armenian mountain spirit Dachnavar similarly sucks blood from the *feet* of wanderers, while Meyer mentions ghostly mothers who suck out the *eyes* of their children. As is well known, toes, feet and eyes are in folklore and mythology, as well as in dreams and psychoneurotic symptoms, frequently recurring phallic symbols. The nervous system, particularly the spinal cord, often has the same symbolic meaning as blood (vital substance), which is the reason why sufferers from excessive nocturnal emissions so often develop the dread of softening of the spine with paralysis. The Roman Strigas, for instance, used to suck, not only the blood of children, but also their spinal marrow. The idea that moral delinquency, essentially masturbation, leads to weakness of the spine is extremely widespread. On the first page of Zschokke's *Die Zauberin Sidonia,* written in 1798, there occurs the following line: "Die Faulheit saugt uns mit ihrem Vampyrenrüssel Mark und Blut ab" ("Laziness with its vampire snout sucks away our marrow and blood"). This may be compared with Jaromir's speech in Grillparzer's *Ahnfrau*:

> Und die Angst mit Vampirrüssel
> Saugt das Blut aus meinen Adern,
> Aus dem Kopfe das Gehirn.

("And terror, with its vampire snout, sucks the blood from out my veins, the brain from out my head.")

It is evident that in the Vampire superstition proper the simple idea of the vital fluid being withdrawn through an exhausting love embrace is complicated by more perverse forms of sexuality, as well as by the admixture of sadism and hate. When the more normal aspects of sexuality are in a state of repression there is always a tendency to regress toward less developed forms. Sadism is one of the chief of these, and it is the earliest form of this—known as oral sadism—that plays such an important part in the Vampire belief. The still earlier stage, the simple sucking that precedes biting, is more connected with the love side we have discussed earlier, the sadism more with the element of hate. The act of sucking has a sexual significance from earliest infancy which is maintained throughout life in the form of kissing; in certain perversions it can actually replace the vagina itself.

From the earliest times myths and legends about Vampires have existed in Europe; a typical example is the Wallachian belief that red-haired men appear after death in the form of frogs, beetles, etc., and drink the blood of beautiful girls. Further, there have come down to us from the earliest Middle Ages reports of the custom—existing in most European countries—of digging up, piercing with a stake or burning the corpse of those spirits who torment the living and suck their blood. As has already been pointed out, this belief is spread over the whole world: for example, the modern Pontianaks of Java, who emanate from corpses, have the habit of sucking blood, and the Assyrian Vampire, called Akakharu, has on the other hand the most ancient lineage. Our fullest knowledge of the belief in Europe, however, we owe to the Balkan peninsula, where it has evidently been greatly influenced by Turkish superstitions. In England we have several complete and typical accounts related by William of Newburgh in the twelfth century, but since that date hardly a trace of the belief is to be found. In ancient Ireland the Vampire, under the name of the Dearg-dul "red blood-sucker," played a considerable part among popular dreads, but he likewise seems to have vanished at an early date.

The epidemics of Vampirism, which had been frequent enough before, reached their highest point in the southeast of Europe during the eighteenth century and lasted well on into the nineteenth. The most alarming took place in Chios in 1708, in Hungary in 1726, in Meduegya and Belgrade in 1725 and 1732, in Servia in 1825, and in Hungary in 1832. In the year 1732 there appeared in Germany alone some fourteen books on the subject, which evoked general horror and drew wide attention to the problem. It did not escape Voltaire's satire, who in his discussion of it in his *Dictionnaire philosophique* wrote: "La difficulté était de savoir si c'était l'âme ou le corps du mort qui mangeait: il fut décidé que c'était l'un et l'autre; les mets délicats et peu substantiels, comme les meringues, la crème fouettée et les fruits fondants, étaient pour l'âme; les ros-bif étaient pour le corps." [3] We are not concerned here with the actual causes of these fatal epidemics, which is a purely medical problem. Hock remarks that they occurred chiefly when plague was rife, and it is certain that the association of stench is common to the two ideas. Bearing in mind the anal-erotic origin of necrophilia, commented on above, we are not surprised to observe what stress many writers on the subject lay on the horrible stink that invests the Vampire. One example of this will suffice: Allacci describes a Greek Vampire called the Burculacas, "than whom no plague more terrible or more harmful to man can well be thought of or conceived. This name is given him from vile filth. For βοῦρκα means bad black mud, not any kind of mud but feculent muck that is slimy and oozing with excrementitious sewerage so that it exhales a most noisome stench. λάκκος is a ditch or a cloaca in which foulness of this kind collects and reeks amain." Plagues, in their turn, have always been associated in the popular—and to some extent in the medical—mind with the notion of stench, particularly from decomposing sewage. The Vampire of Alnwick Castle, whose story is narrated by William of Newburgh, was actually believed to have caused an extensive plague through the evil odors he spread, and it ceased when his corpse was adequately dealt with. The association of ideas explicit in this story was doubtless implicit on countless other occasions. In the Middle Ages there was a close correlation between visitations of the Black Death and outbreaks of Vampirism, and even as late as 1855 the terrible cholera epidemic in Dantsic revived such a widespread belief in the dead returning as Vampires to claim the living that, according to medical opinion, the fears of the people greatly increased the mortality from the disease.

[3] "The difficulty was to determine whether it was the soul or the body of the dead that did the eating: it was decided that it was both; the dishes that were delicate and not very substantial—like meringue, whipped cream, and melting sherbert—were for the soul; the roast beef was for the body" [Editors' translation].

The Vampire superstition is still far from dead in many parts of Europe. In Norway, Sweden and Finland it lasted until quite recently. Krauss reports that at the present day the peasants in Bosnia believe in the existence of Vampires as firmly as in that of God, and the same is hardly less true of the Servian peasant. The belief is still rife in Greece, and Lawson in 1910 says: "Even now a year seldom passes in which some village of Greece does not disembarrass itself of a *vrykolakas* by the traditional means, cremation." In Bulgaria in 1837 a stranger, suspected of being a Vampire, was tortured and burned alive. In 1874, in Rhode Island, U.S.A., a man exhumed the body of his own daughter and burned her heart in the belief that she was endangering the life of other members of the family, and about the same time in Chicago the body of a woman who had died of consumption was dug up and the lungs burned for the same reason. In 1889 in Russia the corpse of an old man, suspected of being a Vampire, was dug up, at which many of those present stoutly maintained they saw a tail attached to his back. In 1899 Roumanian peasants in Krassowa dug up no fewer than thirty corpses and tore them to pieces with the object of stopping an epidemic of diphtheria. Two further instances occurred as recently as 1902, one in Hungary, one in Bucharest, and in 1909 a castle in South Transylvania was burned by the populace, who believed that a Vampire emanating from it was the cause of a sudden increase in the mortality of their children. In 1912 a farmer in Hungary who had suffered from ghostly visitations went to the cemetery one night, stuffed three pieces of garlic—note the homeopathic smell factor in the treatment—and three stones into the mouth, and fixed the corpse to the ground by thrusting a stake through it in the approved fashion.

The word "Vampire" itself, introduced into general European use toward the end of the first third of the eighteenth century, is a Southern Slav word. Its derivation has been much disputed, but the greatest authority, Miklosich, considers the most likely one to be the North Turkish *uber,* a witch. The other Slavonic variants are: Bulgarian and Servian, *vapir;* Polish, *upier;* Russian, *vopyr.* The word has acquired various secondary meanings which are not without interest as showing what significations the conception has for the popular mind. The earliest extension—first made by Buffon—was to designate certain bats which were thought to attack animals and even human beings in sleep. The old idea of a baleful night-flight is plain here. The two chief metaphorical connotations of the word are: (1) a social or political tyrant who sucks the life from his people;

this was used in English as early as 1741; (2) an irresistible lover who sucks away energy, ambition or even life for selfish reasons; the latter may be of either sex, either male, as in Torresani's fascinating cavalry captain, or female, as in Kipling's Vampire poem and in the daily speech of Hollywood.

Nosferatu

JACK KEROUAC

◆◇◆

Nosferatu is an evil name suggesting the red letters of hell—the sinister pieces of it like "fer" and "eratu" and "nos" have a red and heinous quality like the picture itself (which throbs with gloom), a masterpiece of nightmare horror photographed fantastically well in the old grainy tones of brown-and-black-and-white.

It's not so much that the woods are "misty" but that they are bright shining Bavarian woods in the morning as the young jerk hero hurries in a Transylvanian coach to the castle of the Count. Though the woods be bright you feel evil lurking behind every tree. You just know the inner sides of dead trees among the shining living pines have bats hanging upsidedown in torpid sated sleep. There's a castle right ahead. The hero has just had a drink in a Transylvanian tavern and it would be my opinion to suggest "Don't drink too deep in Transylvanian taverns!" The maids in the Inn are as completely innocent as NOSFERATU is completely evil. The horses drawing the coach cavort, the youth stretches in the daytime woods, glad . . . but! . . . *the little traveled road!* The castle coach transfers him at Charlie Chaplin speed to the hungry cardinal of vampires. The horses are hooded! They know that vampire bats will clamp against their withers by nightfall! They rush hysterically through a milky dimming forest of mountain dusk, you suddenly see the castle with bats like flies round the parapet. The kid rushes out looking for to go find his gory boss. In a strange wool cap a thin hawknosed man opens the big oaken door. He announces his servants are all gone. The audience realizes this is Count Nosferatu himself! Ugh! The castle has tile floors:—somehow there's more evil in those tile floors than in the dripping dust of later Bela Lugosi castle where women with spiders on their shoulders dragged dead muslin gowns across the stone. They are the tile floors of a Byzantine Alexandrian Transylvanian throat-ogre.

The Count Nosferatu has the long hook nose of a Javelin vampire bat, the large eyes of the Rhinolophidae vampire bat, long horsey mouth looking like it's full of W-shaped cusps with muggly pectinated teeth and molars and incisors like Desmondontae vampire bats with a front tooth missing the better to suck the blood, maybe with the long brush-tipped tongue of the *sanguisuga* so sanguine. He looks in his hunched swift walk like he probably also has his intestinal tract specially modified in accordance with his nocturnal habits . . . the general horrid hare-lipped look of the Noctilio . . . small guillotines in his mouth . . . the exceeding thinness of his gullet. His hands are like the enormous claws of the Leporinus bat and keep growing longer and longer fingernails throughout the picture.

Meanwhile the kid rushes around enjoying the scenery:—little dusty paths of the castle by day, but by twilight?

The Count plunges to sign his deeds with that thirsty eagerness of the Vampire.

The kid escapes over the wall just in time . . .

The scene shifts to Doktor Van Hellsing in sunny classroom Germany nevertheless photographed as dark as Wolfbane or the claws that eat a fly. Then it goes to a gorgeously filmed dune where women's Victorian dresses flutter in the fresh sea wind. Then finally the haunted ship sails down the navigable canal or river and out to sea: aboard is the Count in pursuit of his boy. When they open his coffin a dozen rats plop out of the dirt and slink and bite the seamen on the ankles (how they ever filmed this I'll never know, great big rats) . . . The whole scene on the ship testifies to the grandeur of the horror of Coleridge's Ancient Mariner. Of itself the schooner glides into the port of Bremen with all the crew dead. The sucked-out Captain is tied to his wheel. A disciple of the Count imprisoned in a Bremen cell sees the schooner glide right by like a ghost and says: "The master is here!" Down cobbles deserted at dusk suddenly, like an insane delivery boy here comes Count Nosferatu carrying his own coffin of burial earth under his arm. He goes straight to establish residence in an eerie awful warehouse or armory which made me think: "I shall never go to Bremen if they have things like that! Armories with empty windows! Ow!"

The old Bremen lamplighter is aware of the foolish hallucinations of Bremen folk but he also looks scared as he lights the evening lamp, naturally, as the next day processions carry the coffined victims of the vampire down the gloomy street. People close their shutters. There is real evil swarming all over the screen by now. Nosferatu looks worse and worse: by now his teeth are stained, his fingernails are like rats' tails, his eyes are on fire. He stares from his warehouse window like someone in an old dream. He rises from his coffin at eve like a plank. His disciple who escapes from the prison looks like Mr. Pickwick on a rampage in a chase that has everybody breathing furiously (a masterpiece of breathing), ends in a field with torches.

At night, by moonlight there he is, the Great Lover, staring across that awful plaza or canal into the heroine's window and into her eye. She waits for him. She wants to save the hero and has read in the "Book of Vampires" that if a victim stays with the vampire till cock's crow he will be destroyed. He comes to her swiftly with that awful quickfooted walk, fingernails dripping. The shadow of the hand crawls like ink across her snowy bedspreads. The last scene shows him kneeling at her bedside kissing into her neck in a horribly perverted love scene unequalled for its pathetic sudden revelation of the vampire's essential helplessness. The sun comes up, you see its rays light the top of his warehouse, the cock crows, he can't get away. He vanishes in a puff of smoke like the Agony of the West. Right there on the floor as the puffing hero arrives too late to save his love.

The creator of this picture, F. W. Murnau, may have drawn a lot of information from the great vampire dissertations of Ranft and Calmet written in the 18th century. Vampire is a word of Servian origin (Wampir),—meaning blood-sucking ghosts. They were supposed to be the souls of dead wizards and witches and suicides and victims of homicide and the Banished! (those banished from family or church). But vampires were also thought to be the souls of ordinary living people which leave the body in sleep and come upon other sleepers in the form of down-fluff! . . . so don't sleep in your duck-down sleepingbag in Transylvania! (or even in California, they say).

Actually, don't worry . . . scientifically speaking, the only blood-sucking bats in the world are located in South America from Oaxaca on down.

Frankenstein Meets the Edison Company

◆◆

In 1910 the Edison Company released a 700-foot-long version of Mary Shelley's famous novel. Unfortunately nothing of the film survives except a few stills and a photograph of the monster (played by an unnamed actor) on the cover of the Edison catalogue. Luckily the extant press releases for the film contain not only a colorful synopsis of the action but also both a scenario and a musical accompaniment cue sheet.

Film historians sometimes refer to the Edison Company's *Frankenstein* as the "first monster movie." (The icicle-bedecked, man-eating giant in Melies's *Conquest of the Pole* actually made his debut two years later.) Despite all the disclaimers in the publicity that harrowing effects had been scrupulously avoided, the surviving stills, as well as the bare bones of the scenario, indicate an element of intentional terror and suspense. At any rate, as the reader will see from the press release and scenario reprinted below, the Edison *Frankenstein* was probably an extraordinary film—with its complex mirror sequence and *doppelgänger* motif suggestive of the German expressionistic school, its use of tinted film stock to give atmospheric effects, and its long sequence of cross-cuts between Frankenstein and the smoking vat, giving a James Whale kind of suspense to the creation episode.

FROM THE PRESS RELEASE, FEBRUARY, 14, 1910 [1]

. . . In making the film the Edison Company has carefully tried to eliminate all the actually repulsive situations, and to concentrate upon the mystic and psychological problems that are to be found in

---

[1] From the Museum of Modern Art Archives.

this weird tale. Wherever, therefore, the film differs from the original story, it is purely with the idea of eliminating what would be repulsive to a moving picture audience.

. . . The story of the film brings out the fact that the creation of the monster was only possible because Frankenstein had allowed his normal mind to be overcome by evil and unnatural thoughts.

. . . With the strength of Frankenstein's love for his bride and the effect of this upon his own mind, the monster cannot exist. Therefore, from this comes the reason for the next and closing scene which has probably never been surpassed in anything shown on the moving picture screen. The monster broken down by his unsuccessful attempts to be with his creator enters the room, stands before a large mirror holding out his arms entreatingly, but gradually the real monster fades away, leaving only the image in the mirror. A moment later Frankenstein enters.

Standing directly before the mirror we see the remarkable sight of the monster's image reflected instead of Frankenstein's own. Gradually, however, under the effect of love and his better nature, the monster's image fades and Frankenstein sees himself in his young manhood in the mirror. His bride joins him, and the film ends with their embrace, Frankenstein's mind now being clear of the awful horror and weight it has been laboring under for so long.

SCENARIO

Subtitle: "Frankenstein leaves for college."

Scene 1: *Room-Interior.* Frankenstein leaves.

Subtitle: "Two years later. Frankenstein has discovered the mystery of life."

Scene 2: *Laboratory.* Frankenstein gets a great idea and experiments.

Subtitle: "Just before the experiment."

Scene 3: *Interior of bed room.* Frankenstein writes letter. *Orange and yellow tint.*

Scene 3a: *The letter:*
"Sweetheart,

Tonight my ambition will be accomplished. I have discovered the secret of life and death, and in a few hours I shall create into life the most perfect human being that the world has yet known. When this marvellous work is accomplished I shall then return to claim you for my bride.

Your devoted,

Frankenstein."

Scene 4: *Room-Interior.* Frankenstein leaves with candle. *Orange and yellow.*

Subtitle: "Instead of a perfect human being the evil in Frankenstein's mind creates a monster."

Scene 5: *Room-Interior,* showing the vat. Frankenstein pours in fluid. *Orange and yellow.*

Scene 6: *Vat* showing smoke. *Orange and yellow.*

Scene 7: *Room-Interior,* showing the doors of the vat. Frankenstein looks in. *Orange and yellow.*

Scene 8: *Vat.* Monster forming. *Orange and yellow.*

[Scenes 9 through 17 alternate between Frankenstein looking into the vat and the monster forming. *Orange and yellow.*]

Scene 18: *Vat.* Monster formed. *Orange and yellow.*

Scene 19: *Room-Interior,* showing the head of monster coming through the door.

Subtitle: "Frankenstein appalled at the sight of his evil creation."

Scene 20: *Room-Interior.* Frankenstein, while asleep, sees monster. *Orange and yellow.*

Subtitle: "The return home."

Scene 21: *Room-Interior.* Frankenstein returns.

Subtitle: "Haunting his creator and jealous of his sweetheart, for the first time the monster sees himself."

Scene 22: *Room-Interior.* Frankenstein sees monster. Monster sees himself in glass and struggles with Frankenstein tearing from his waistcoat the flower that his fiancée had given him.

Subtitle: "On the bridal night Frankenstein's better nature asserting itself."

Scene 23: *Room-Interior.* Frankenstein congratulated by his friends. *Orange and yellow.*

Scene 24: *Room-Interior.* Frankenstein goes out with light and monster enters. *Blue.*

Subtitle: "The creation of an evil mind is overcome by love and
    disappears."
Scene 25: *Room-Interior.* Monster seeing his vision in glass
        disappears. Frankenstein's mind becomes peaceful.
        Orange and yellow.

The End

The Monster's Lost Paradise
MARY SHELLEY

◆◆

*After several months' absence, the monster returns to his creator,
Victor Frankenstein, and recounts his adventures.*
". . . I entered a barn which had appeared to me to be empty.
A woman was sleeping on some straw; she was young, of an agreeable
aspect, and blooming in the loveliness of youth and health. Here, I
thought, is one of those whose joy-imparting smiles are bestowed
on all but me. And then I bent over her, and whispered, 'Awake,
fairest, thy lover is near—he who would give his life but to obtain
one look of affection from thine eyes: my beloved, awake!'
"The sleeper stirred; a thrill of terror ran through me. . . . She
moved again, and I fled. . . .
"What I ask of you is reasonable and moderate; I demand a creature of another sex, but as hideous as myself; the gratification is
small, but it is all that I can receive, and it shall content me. It is
true, we shall be monsters, cut off from all the world; but on that
account we shall be more attached to one another. Our lives will not
be happy, but they will be harmless, and free from the misery I now
feel. Oh! my creator, make me happy; let me feel gratitude towards
you for one benefit! Let me see that I excite the sympathy of some
existing thing; do not deny me my request!"
I was moved. I shuddered when I thought of the possible conse-
quences of my consent; but I felt that there was some justice in his
argument. His tale, and the feelings he now expressed, proved him

From the novel Frankenstein. *First published in England in 1818.*

to be a creature of fine sensations; and did I not, as his maker, owe him all the portion of happiness that it was in my power to bestow? He saw my change of feeling, and continued—

"If you consent, neither you nor any other human being shall ever see us again: I will go to the vast wilds of South America. My food is not that of man; I do not destroy the lamb and the kid to glut my appetite; acorns and berries afford me sufficient nourishment. My companion will be of the same nature as myself, and will be content with the same fare. We shall make our bed of dried leaves; the sun will shine on us as on man, and will ripen our food. The picture I present to you is peaceful and human, and you must feel that you could deny it only in the wantonness of power and cruelty. Pitiless as you have been towards me, I now see compassion in your eyes; let me seize the favourable moment, and persuade you to promise what I so ardently desire. . . ."

"I consent to your demand, on your solemn oath to quit Europe for ever, and every other place in the neighbourhood of man, as soon as I shall deliver into your hands a female who will accompany you in your exile."

"I swear," he cried, "by the sun, and by the blue sky of Heaven, and by the fire of love that burns my heart, that if you grant my prayer, while they exist you shall never behold me again. . . ."

I packed up my chemical instruments, and the materials I had collected, resolving to finish my labours in some obscure nook in the northern highlands of Scotland. . . . I did not doubt but that the monster followed me, and would discover himself to me when I should have finished, that he might receive his companion.

With this resolution I traversed the northern highlands, and fixed on one of the remotest of the Orkneys as the scene of my labours. It was a place fitted for such a work, being hardly more than a rock, whose high sides were continually beaten upon by the waves. The soil was barren, scarcely affording pasture for a few miserable cows, and oatmeal for its inhabitants, which consisted of five persons, whose gaunt and scraggy limbs gave tokens of their miserable fare. Vegetables and bread, when they indulged in such luxuries, and even fresh water, was to be procured from the main land, which was about five miles distant.

On the whole island there were but three miserable huts, and one of these was vacant when I arrived. This I hired. It contained but two rooms, and these exhibited all the squalidness of the most miserable penury. The thatch had fallen in, the walls were unplastered, and the door was off its hinges. I ordered it to be repaired, bought some furniture, and took possession; an incident which would, doubtless, have occasioned some surprise, had not all the senses of the cottagers been benumbed by want and squalid poverty. As it was, I lived ungazed at and unmolested, hardly thanked for the pittance of food and clothes which I gave; so much does suffering blunt even the coarsest sensations of men.

In this retreat I devoted the morning to labour; but in the evening, when the weather permitted, I walked on the stony beach of the sea, to listen to the waves as they roared and dashed at my feet. It was a monotonous yet ever-changing scene. I thought of Switzerland; it was far different from this desolate and appalling landscape. Its hills are covered with vines, and its cottages are scattered thickly in the plains. Its fair lakes reflect a blue and gentle sky; and, when troubled by the winds, their tumult is but as the play of a lively infant, when compared to the roarings of the giant ocean.

In this manner I distributed my occupations when I first arrived; but, as I proceeded in my labour, it became every day more horrible and irksome to me. Sometimes I could not prevail on myself to enter my laboratory for several days; and at other times I toiled day and night in order to complete my work. It was, indeed, a filthy process in which I was engaged. During my first experiment, a kind of enthusiastic frenzy had blinded me to the horror of my employment; my mind was intently fixed on the consummation of my labour, and my eyes were shut to the horror of my proceedings. But now I went to it in cold blood, and my heart often sickened at the work of my hands.

Thus situated, employed in the most detestable occupation, immersed in a solitude where nothing could for an instant call my attention from the actual scene in which I was engaged, my spirits became unequal; I grew restless and nervous. Every moment I feared to meet my persecutor. Sometimes I sat with my eyes fixed on the ground, fearing to raise them, lest they should encounter the object which I so much dreaded to behold. I feared to wander from the sight of my fellow-creatures, lest when alone he should come to claim his companion.

In the mean time I worked on, and my labour was already considerably advanced. I looked towards its completion with a tremulous and eager hope, which I dared not trust myself to question, but which was intermixed with obscure forebodings of evil, that made my heart sicken in my bosom.

I sat one evening in my laboratory; the sun had set, and the moon was just rising from the sea; I had not sufficient light for my employment, and I remained idle, in a pause of consideration of whether I should leave my labour for the night, or hasten its conclusion by an unremitting attention to it. As I sat, a train of reflection occurred to me, which led me to consider the effects of what I was now doing. Three years before I was engaged in the same manner, and had created a fiend whose unparalleled barbarity had desolated my heart, and filled it for ever with the bitterest remorse. I was now about to form another being, of whose dispositions I was alike ignorant; she might become ten thousand times more malignant than her mate, and delight, for its own sake, in murder and wretchedness. He had sworn to quit the neighbourhood of man, and hide himself in deserts; but she had not; and she, who in all probability was to become a thinking and reasoning animal, might refuse to comply with a compact made before her creation. They might even hate each other; the creature who already lived loathed his own deformity, and might he not conceive a greater abhorrence for it when it came before his eyes in the female form? She also might turn with disgust from him to the superior beauty of man; she might quit him, and he be again alone, exasperated by the fresh provocation of being deserted by one of his own species.

Even if they were to leave Europe, and inhabit the deserts of the new world, yet one of the first results of those sympathies for which the dæmon thirsted would be children, and a race of devils would be propagated upon the earth, who might make the very existence of the species of man a condition precarious and full of terror. Had I a right, for my own benefit, to inflict this curse upon everlasting generations? I had before been moved by the sophisms of the being I had created; I had been struck senseless by his fiendish threats: but now, for the first time, the wickedness of my promise burst upon me; I shuddered to think that future ages might curse me as their pest, whose selfishness had not hesitated to buy its own peace at the price, perhaps, of the existence of the whole human race.

I trembled, and my heart failed within me; when, on looking up, I saw, by the light of the moon, the dæmon at the casement. A ghastly grin wrinkled his lips as he gazed on me, where I sat fulfilling the task which he had allotted to me. Yes, he had followed me in my travels; he had loitered in forests, hid himself in caves, or taken refuge in wide and desert heaths; and he now came to mark my progress, and claim the fulfillment of my promise.

As I looked on him, his countenance expressed the utmost extent of malice and treachery. I thought with a sensation of madness on my promise of creating another like to him, and trembling with passion, tore to pieces the thing on which I was engaged. The wretch saw me destroy the creature on whose future existence he depended for happiness, and, with a howl of devilish despair and revenge, withdrew.

I left the room, and, locking the door, made a solemn vow in my own heart never to resume my labours; and then, with trembling steps, I sought my own apartment. I was alone; none were near me to dissipate the gloom, and relieve me from the sickening oppression of the most terrible reveries.

Several hours passed, and I remained near my window gazing on the sea; it was almost motionless, for the winds were hushed, and all nature reposed under the eye of the quiet moon. A few fishing vessels alone specked the water, and now and then the gentle breeze wafted the sound of voices, as the fishermen called to one another. I felt the silence, although I was hardly conscious of its extreme profundity, until my ear was suddenly arrested by the paddling of oars near the shore, and a person landed close to my house.

In a few minutes after, I heard the creaking of my door, as if some one endeavoured to open it softly. I trembled from head to foot; I felt a presentiment of who it was, and wished to rouse one of the peasants who dwelt in a cottage not far from mine; but I was overcome by the sensation of helplessness, so often felt in frightful dreams, when you in vain endeavour to fly from an impending danger, and was rooted to the spot.

Presently I heard the sound of footsteps along the passage; the door opened, and the wretch whom I dreaded appeared. Shutting the door, he approached me, and said, in a smothered voice—

"You have destroyed the work which you began; what is it that you intend? Do you dare to break your promise? I have endured toil and misery: I left Switzerland with you; I crept along the shores of the Rhine, among its willow islands, and over the summits of its hills. I have dwelt many months in the heaths of England, and among the deserts of Scotland. I have endured incalculable fatigue, and cold, and hunger; do you dare destroy my hopes?"

"Begone! I do break my promise; never will I create another like yourself, equal in deformity and wickedness."

"Slave, I before reasoned with you, but you have proved yourself unworthy of my condescension. Remember that I have power; you believe yourself miserable, but I can make you so wretched that the light of day will be hateful to you. You are my creator, but I am your master;—obey!"

"The hour of my irresolution is past, and the period of your power is arrived. Your threats cannot move me to do an act of wickedness; but they confirm me in a determination of not creating you a companion in vice. Shall I, in cool blood, set loose upon the earth a dæmon, whose delight is in death and wretchedness? Begone! I am firm, and your words will only exasperate my rage."

The monster saw my determination in my face, and gnashed his teeth in the impotence of anger.

"Shall each man," cried he, "find a wife for his bosom, and each beast have his mate, and I be alone? I had feelings of affection, and they were requited by detestation and scorn. Man! you may hate; but beware! your hours will pass in dread and misery, and soon the bolt will fall which must ravish from you your happiness for ever. Are you to be happy, while I grovel in the intensity of my wretchedness? You can blast my other passions; but revenge remains—revenge, henceforth dearer than light or food! I may die; but first you, my tyrant and tormentor, shall curse the sun that gazes on your misery. Beware; for I am fearless, and therefore powerful. I will watch with the wiliness of a snake, that I may sting with its venom. Man, you shall repent of the injuries you inflict."

"Devil, cease; and do not poison the air with these sounds of malice. I have declared my resolution to you, and I am no coward to bend beneath words. Leave me; I am inexorable."

"It is well. I go; but remember, I shall be with you on your wedding-night."

Almost Eve: The Creation Scene
in *The Bride of Frankenstein*
ROY HUSS

Although it is a commonplace to point out that James Whale's second Frankenstein feature was both a parody and satire of his first, it would be foolish to think that all *The Bride of Frankenstein* has to offer is an ephemeral delight in "high camp." A good satirist, as Max Beerbohm pointed out, is (unless he be a Swiftian misanthrope) in love with the objects of his barbs; and his being a successful parodist, as Beerbohm also reminded us, is completely dependent upon his ability to suffuse his own tone and style with that of the original. Since Whale himself is the *auteur* he is parodying and satirizing, this was of course a simple task.

Whale's second Frankenstein film is therefore both ironical and unironical. His frequent use of the tilted camera in the "creation scene" is equivalent to placing the ponderously serious scientific preoccupations of Drs. Frankenstein and Pretorius before a distorting mirror in a funhouse. Yet, at the same time, he brings us into an intense, suspenseful involvement with the "reality" of creating the "bride." This is due primarily to his brilliant technique of editing the sequence, the flavor of which I have tried to convey in the following shot analysis.

A couple of remarks about the content of the episode. Whale's apparent emphasis on the gimmickry and gadgetry of the feverish laboratory activity which brings the monster's "bride" to life would seem to place the sequence within the exclusive purview of the science fiction enthusiast. Yet the "hardware" is by itself of little interest. (Studying the scenes through a viewer, I was surprised at the primitive construction of some of the equipment: a simple birdcage device containing an oversized light bulb; an upright platform with large shock absorber springs attached; large porcelain resistors, and so on.) Rather, one's scientific interest is quickly overcome by the apprehension about whether the unleashed energy—both natural lightning and manmade electricity (seeming more like Doomsday than Creation)—can be contained by the apparatus. Will these equivalents of the divine Promethean fire animate dead atoms or reduce everything to atomic ashes (as in fact happens at the film's end, when the monster pulls the mysterious "destruct" lever)? Our fear of unknown or incalcuable forces overwhelms any respect for the scientific ingenuity that invokes them. This places the sequence, and the film in general, into the horror rather than into the science fiction genre.

Another peculiar aspect of the content of the creation sequence in *The Bride of Frankenstein* is its relation to its somewhat remote source in Mary Shelley's novel. In some ways it seems as if Whale were trying, in spite of his satiric undertone, to bring his sequel closer than his first film to the spirit of its literary inspiration. One

obvious bit of evidence for this, of course, is his prologue recalling
the circumstances of the novel's conception: the birth of the idea on
a stormy night in Switzerland in the company of Shelley and Byron.
The other influence is less palpable but more effective as well as affecting: the transformation of the monster into an accursed but pitiable Adam, one who ascends the human scale, though he is still
grotesque, first by gaining the power of speech (in the novel by
secretly observing a peasant family; in the film by being tutored
by a blind shepherd), then by desiring a mate. Although the Dr.
Frankenstein of the novel destroys the female monster before endow-
ing it with life and the Dr. Frankenstein of the film, on the other
hand, gives her a few moments of existence before the monster destroys her, along with himself and Dr. Pretorius, Whale nevertheless
conforms to the novel by dramatizing one of the projected fears of
Mary Shelley's protagonist. The female monster might, Victor Frankenstein reasoned, "refuse to comply with a compact made before her
creation. . . . She also might turn with disgust from him [the male
monster] to the superior beauty of man. . . ." In the sequence immediately following the one analyzed below, the "bride" (played by
Elsa Lanchester) fulfills this prophecy with a vengeance: she emits
a piercing scream at the sight of her proposed "groom" (Boris Karloff) and makes tracks immediately for the handsome form and
countenance of her youthful creator.

One final point of contact between the sequence described below
and the novel should be mentioned. Whereas Mary Shelley prevents
her hero from speaking about the scientific process by which he
creates both the monster and his mate, merely referring in the
vaguest terms to Frankenstein's "chemical apparatus," Whale transforms the experiment into one of the most impressive pyrotechnic
displays on film. Yet even in this, the two *auteurs* were more in
harmony than they seemed, for in her preface to *Frankenstein* Mary
Shelley revealed a vision closer to Whale's, one from which he may
actually have taken a few hints:

> Not thus [by biochemical means], after all, would life be given.
> Perhaps a corpse would be re-animated; galvanism had given a
> token of such things: perhaps the component parts of a creature
> might be manufactured, brought together, and endued with vital
> warmth. . . . I saw—with shut eyes, but acute mental vision, . . .
> the hideous phantom of a man stretched out, and then, on the
> working of some powerful engine, show signs of life, and stir with
> an uneasy, half vital motion.

SHOT ANALYSIS

SCENE: DR. FRANKENSTEIN'S CASTLE AT NIGHT

Shot no. 1. In Frankenstein's laboratory Dr. Pretorius, *at left of frame* and in *medium-long shot,* runs *diagonally to the right toward the camera.* The *camera tracks and pans with him to the right* until he arrives at *medium close-up.* (Dr. Frankenstein can be seen sitting at his desk at the back of the laboratory.) Pretorius stops at a table filled with chemical and electrical apparatus. *The camera dollies and pans around* him *a few degrees.* Frankenstein runs from the rear of the lab toward the table.

> *Comment:* In typical suspense-action films the rule is to begin quietly and end with a "cut on the action." Whale frequently reverses this, as he has here. Opening with the sight of old Pretorius running adds an unexpected freneticism. The diagonal direction of movement (like any diagonal line in plastic art) adds a sense of excitement as well as ties together background and foreground. The slight revolving of the camera around the table, while the panning keeps the apparatus in the center of the frame, causes a parallax of other objects in the lab. This not only increases the three-dimensional effect of the tableau but also highlights the table as a center of interest—the origin of the "bride's" life.

   Cut to:

2. *Close-up* of a dial recording the beat of a heart taken from an exhumed corpse. *Cut to:*

3. *Close-up* of Pretorious, facing right. *The camera is tilted to the right at a sharp angle,* so that Pretorius seems to be leaning left.

Comment: Whale's occasional use of this device throughout the sequence is his main means of asserting his satirical voice. This technique was later imitated for similar reasons in films like *Holiday for Henrietta* and the popular Batman series on television.

Pretorius: "The heart is beating more regularly now."
   Cut to:

4. *Close-up* of Frankenstein facing left, this time *the camera being
   tilted to the left.*

Frankenstein: "Yes, it's been beating for nine hours. . . . Not yet,
but soon."

   Cut to:

5. *Extreme close-up* of Pretorius, *the camera tilted with greater
   exaggeration to the right.*
   Pretorius: "And the brain?"

   Cut to:

6. *Close-up* of Frankenstein, facing left, *camera tilted left* (as in
   shot 4)
   Frankenstein: "Perfect. And already in position." . . .

9. *Close-up* of Pretorius, facing right, *camera tilted right* (as in
   shot 3).
   Pretorius: "Shall we put the heart in now?"

   Cut to:

10. *Medium two-shot* of Frankenstein and Pretorius (pieces of ap-
    paratus surrounding them). They look off-screen to the right,
    camera tilted to the right.
    Frankenstein: "Yes. Ludwig!"

Frankenstein rises from his chair as an assistant enters screen
right. The three men move the table with its apparatus to the right
—*the camera panning with them*—near the table where the as yet
unanimated "bride" lies wrapped in bandages.

   Cut to:

11. *Medium two-shot, the camera still tilted right,* of Frankenstein
    and the assistant arranging instruments on the table. *The cam-
    era dollies in for a close-up* of Frankenstein.
    Frankenstein: "It's beating quite normally now. Bring it over."

The camera tilts down to Frankenstein's hand on the table. The
hand then slides off the table as Frankenstein walks off-screen to
the left.

Comment: Whale's mastery of a scene is evident in this shot, in
which the close-up of Frankenstein's hands functions both as syn-
ecdoche (the part standing for the whole) and as litotes (dramatic
understatement). Later parallel shots focusing on the hands of
Frankenstein and Pretorius (highlighting the sources of creation),
the hands of the "bride" (trembling with the galvanizing energy),

and the hands of the monster (caressing those of his mate) speak an eloquent cinematic "body language."

   Cut to:

12. *Medium shot, camera tilted right,* of Pretorius leaning over the chemical equipment. The "bride" can be seen lying on the table in the background. Frankenstein enters screen right. Pretorius and Frankenstein go to the "bride," Pretorius carrying a jar of dark liquid. Pretorius turns as . . .

   Cut to:

13. *Reverse angle medium two-shot* of Pretorius and Frankenstein leaning over "bride." Pretorius lifts up a heart with pincers.

   Quick dissolve to:

14. *Exterior, medium-long shot* of top of tower—a cloud-covered, windswept nighttime sky, fires burning on turrets—flashes of lightning.

   Quick dissolve to:

15. *Interior, medium shot* of dark dungeon doorway. Against the background of a lightning flash reflected in the corridor, Ludwig, the assistant, rushes in, moving obliquely toward camera (*medium shot to close-up*).

  Ludwig: "The storm is rising."

   Cut to:

16. *Medium two-shot, the camera at eyelevel,* of Pretorius and Frankenstein preparing the "bride."

   Cut to:

17. *Close-up* of hands removing sheet from "bride's" bandaged face.

   Cut to:

18. *Medium close-up, bust shot* of Pretorius and Frankenstein, a chain suspended between them.

  Pretorius: "It's amazing, Henry. Lying here in this skull is an artificially developed human brain. Each cell, each convolution ready, waiting for life to come."

   Cut to:

19. *Close-up* of bandaged face of "bride" in profile. The caressing hand of Pretorius enters frame from left.

   Cut to:

20. *Medium close-up* of Pretorius and Frankenstein (as in shot 18).

  Pretorius: "Look! The storm is coming up over the mountains. It'll be here soon."

Cut to:

21. *Medium shot* of Gothic window of laboratory, lightning seen without, jars on the left in foreground.

    Cut to:

22. *Medium shot* of Pretorius and Frankenstein (as in shots 18 and 20). Pretorius looks obliquely toward the left.
    Frankenstein: "The kites! Are the kites ready?"

    Cut to:

23. *Medium shot* of Ludwig entering (as in shot 15).
    Ludwig: "Yes!"

    Cut to:

24. *Medium shot* of Frankenstein and Pretorius hovering over the "bride" (as before).
    Frankenstein: "Then send them up as soon as the wind rises. Hurry!"
    Pretorius moves off-screen left.

    Cut to:

25. *Upward-tilted close-up* of grimacing face of Ludwig looking obliquely right, his hand cupping his mouth, in order to be heard over the sound of the rising storm.

    Comment: This recalls a device characteristic of German silent films; i.e., sound being suggested by framing its source at close quarters at an unusual angle.

    Ludwig: "The kites, the kites! Get 'em ready!" . . .

29. *Medium shot* of Frankenstein and Pretorius turning on electrical equipment. They run off-screen left, leaving an electric arc device operating in the center of the frame. The "bride's" head can be seen in rear.

    Cut to:

30–36. More electrical equipment begins to operate.
    Frankenstein's voice: "It's coming up!"
    Thunder and lightning.

    Cut to:

37. *Medium-long shot* of the head of Pretorius at bottom of frame, surrounded by flashing devices—explosive burst of light.

    Comment: Here the shots are cut into a staccato rhythm both to suggest the characteristics of the lightning, upon which the whole experiment depends and to highlight the feverish activity of the "creators."

49–57. More shots of preparations for elevating the platform containing the "bride" to the roof. *Long shots* from roof opening to platform. *Reverse angle shots* from floor to roof opening as platform rises upward away from camera. Sparks falling.

58. Exterior. *Medium-long shot* of kites being struck by lightning. . . .

70. The device is lowered back into the laboratory.
    Cut to:

71. *Medium shot, eyelevel,* from feet of "bride," of Frankenstein and Pretorius ministering to the body.
    Pretorius: "Remove the diffuser bands."
    The electrodes are removed from her head.
    Cut to:

72. *Close-up* of "bride's" trembling hand. Another hand reaches into the frame from the left to touch it. . . .

78. *Extreme close-up* of open eyes of "bride" looking through slit in bandages.
    Cut to:

79. *Close-up* of Frankenstein's face.
    Frankenstein: "She's alive! ALIVE!"
    Cut to:

80. *Medium-long shot* of Frankenstein and Pretorius scurrying around "bride." They flip table top, with "bride" strapped to it, to upright position. *The camera dollies in fast.*
    Cut to:

81. *Close-up, bust shot* of "bride."
    Cut to:

82. *Close-up* of Frankenstein's face.
    Cut to:

83. *Close-up* of Pretorius's face.
    Cut to:

84. *Close-up, bust shot* of "bride" (as in shot 81). She lowers her arms.
    Cut to:

85. *Extreme close-up* of "bride's" bandaged face, her opened eyes

showing through the bandages. Her head sags in a swoon. Hands reach in from each side of the frame in order to lift the head.

Cut to:

86. *Medium shot* of the same scene as above.

Cut to:

87. *Medium-long shot* of the "bride" groomed for a wedding. She stands in the center, her hair protruding straight up, in a parody of Nefertiti. A loose gown hastily draped over her remaining bandages flairs out to the left. She is flanked by her "fathers," Frankenstein and Pretorius, as if posing for an official wedding photograph.

Cut to:

88–90. Successive *"portrait" close-ups* of the "bride's" head from *different angles, the camera tilted upward.*

Cut to:

91. *Medium close-up* of Pretorius, who announces to the accompaniment of triumphal music and wedding bells: "The Bride of Frankenstein!"

Modern Gothic

Jekyll and Hyde and the Cruel Cinema
MICHEL PEREZ

❖❖❖

Victor Fleming's 1941 film version of *Dr. Jekyll and Mr. Hyde*
surprises us first of all in being so good. Made under the paternal
auspices of Louis B. Mayer, a man with an eye prudishly keen
enough to detect to the hundreth of a millimeter the least flash of
undraped flesh; directed by a man whose claims to glory rest on
that masterpiece among ladies' pictures *Gone with the Wind* and
some happy incursions into fairyland like *The Wizard of Oz;* photographed by specialists in that mellow Victorian light one used to see
bathing the ingénue brows of the four dear girls of *Little Women,*
or else illuminating the pre-Raphaelite sensuality of Jeanette Mac-
donald; played by a stocky little man with a warm, open smile and
a Swedish actress bursting with health who had formerly shown at
best an aptitude for playing nurses and dreamy violinists—*Dr.
Jekyll and Mr. Hyde* nonetheless triumphs over these daunting circumstances.

Fleming's movie is of course a re-make of Rouben Mamoulian's
1932 film. We saw the latter again recently, and it eclipsed the memory of Fleming's. We admired Mamoulian's lucidity, his unfailing
skill in mastering the most theatrical situations, and his curious
power of working a sort of expressionist magic, using the obvious
excesses proper to horror stories and the lyric effusions of opera.

But the re-release of the Fleming version is timely, all the more so
with the new wind now blowing and with only the maddest extrem-
ists still refusing to admit the limitations of the *auteur* theory in

From Positif, *no. 76 (June, 1966): 130–34. Copyright © 1966 by
Editions le Terrain Vague. English translation by J. D. Allen. Copyright © 1972 by J. D. Allen. Used by permission of the publisher and
the translator.*

evaluating American films, especially those of the thirties. If one is willing to risk granting Mamoulian the status of an *auteur,* and a misunderstood *auteur* at that, one surely wants to accord the same honor to Fleming, a man who was once assistant to D. W. Griffith, and who was probably responsible for that delightful film out of the Griffith stable, *Nightmares and Superstitions;* but who, for all that, still remains one of the old faithfuls of the Metro system. Fleming followed orders. His successes are team successes, and his failures, like *Tortilla Flat,* team failures.

Dr. Jekyll and Mr. Hyde succeeds because the limits imposed by the producer proved a creative spur to the craftsman. The film is excellent not despite the Metro company but because of it.

In Mamoulian's work Miriam Hopkins plays a mildly perverse young woman who pleases Hyde because of what he takes to be her depraved tastes. She is a kindred spirit, first a companion in vice, then a victim. But in Fleming's version, the Hopkins role now played by Ingrid Bergman gives us a type that is complementary not to Hyde but to Jekyll! We see Bergman as a waitress, a somewhat giddy female who ought never to have left her father's farm. This awkward dance-hall girl can't even pour champagne. She is as ill-at-ease in the whirl of night life as is Jekyll, brooding on the savagery of his own imagination. Although the waitress does not appear in Stevenson's story, no more than does the doctor's young society fiancée (these two roles probably deriving from the earliest adaptations of *The Strange Case of Dr. Jekyll and Mr. Hyde,* the best known of which starred John Barrymore), she adds greatly to both films and especially improves Fleming's, giving it a sharp and original flavor. In the Mamoulian work, made at Paramount and dating from that extraordinary heyday of the pre-Hays "talkie," the female lead is more unabashedly erotic.

Yet Fleming's characters are far more disturbing since they are closer to us and more familiar—creatures of a quasi-realist adventure. We are struck by how much Mayer's own Victorianism matches the tone of this Victorian work. Ingrid Bergman projects that love of life which is frowned upon by the puritan conscience and which Stevenson's Jekyll considers the worst of his criminal compulsions. But to us nothing seems more monstrous than this aversion itself, especially in view of the poor girl who smells so much of fresh hay that we would not be surprised to see real cherries on her hat.

Hyde of course has a zestful taste for debauchery. His youthful fervor and lust for pleasure are not simply "egotistical," however: they reflect a gargantuan vitality, as is suggested by the hair covering his face and limbs; by his light and bounding step; by his rediscovered youth. Traditionally, Hyde is made up to appear older than Jekyll, an error due to the conventions of horror films. Actually, Stevenson described Hyde as younger, and perhaps handsomer; the terror he arouses does not come from the deformity of his features but from what one can read there: the expression of pure amorality. And the fascination he exerts over his victims resembles that of Dorian Gray, another representative type of Victorian bad boy. (In this connection we should recall Terence Fisher's astonishing adaptation of the story. For the first time Hyde is presented as more attractive than Jekyll; after he is hunted down, and as he accuses Jekyll of the crimes imputed to him, his features decompose to reveal the face of "the horrible doctor.") Even so, Tracy's make-up is almost flattering in that it does not deform Jekyll's face but merely gives it the cast of a libertine.

Bergman desires Jekyll. She desires the good, the beautiful, the respectable. She loves Jekyll but as Jekyll himself loves the good, the beautiful, the respectable. Jekyll is in love with himself, just as every puritan is in love with the role he has chosen to play in the social comedy. Hyde pursues Jekyll with both hatred and love. And Jekyll can find no way of refusing Hyde. So too Bergman yields to her bondage with a somber joy, and reveals her secret to us in the course of a frantic monologue describing her masochistic fantasies about what Hyde might do to her if she attempted to break free of him. She plays the only game worth playing, as the social comedy gives way to a theater of phantoms. Bergman's inspired acting in this scene and the Metro cameraman's brilliant play of light are enough to give us the message.

Set designers, cameramen, costumers, make-up men, actors—all surpass themselves in the sequences which take place in Hyde's apartment. Here at last is cruel cinema rather than an academic "cinema of cruelty." (Yet who would have thought to look to the cinema for an illustration of certain pages from *The Story of O*?) Drugged with pleasure and fear, having become as much an animal as Hyde, eyes bovine, flesh bruised and softened, mouth perpetually half open, Bergman sleepwalks. She staggers about in torn lace, tripping over refuse strewn on the floor. Hyde spits grape skins, hurls knick-knacks at random, dashes wine in her face. The rising odor of rottenness, life a hundred times more intense and pleasure a hundred times more vivid, hasten the dissolution toward which the film accelerates at each gesture, at each movement of fear and hope. This is not the sort of thing we either expect or find in the standard horror film, which merely rattles a few skeletons and offers some tokens of horror, never this physical reality of pain and terror.

The script-writers have dealt with Stevenson's fable in an appropriately inspired manner. There is of course the gratuitous opening, when we learn that Jekyll could not bring himself to continue his work were it not for his passion to ease the suffering of humanity by helping the mentally ill. Contemporary hypocrisy this, since, as a good Victorian, the original Jekyll permits himself no humanitarian excuses but seeks only to create a double to bear the blame for the shameful pleasures which he already knows he cannot renounce. But the film recaptures the tale's full ambiguity in the admirable scenes when Hyde, at the piano in Bergman's flat, recognizes Jekyll's gestures. It is the cultivated Jekyll who is playing the piano, not the animal Hyde. When Jekyll is on the way to the house of his innocent fiancée, it is Hyde who whistles the melody identified with Bergman. It is in such moments that the cinema displays its power to make us *feel* what was no more than intellectual speculation in the English novelist. In the long line of Jekyll and Hyde movies, we must single out Fleming's, which rises far above the theatrical and decorative preoccupations of horror-film hacks.

Eyes without a Face
RAYMOND DURGNAT

❖❖❖

By his reckless driving, a brilliant plastic surgeon, Dr. Genessier (Pierre Brasseur), is responsible for disfiguring his daughter Christiane (Edith Scob). Unaccustomed to being "contradicted" by fate, he resolves to confer a new face on his daughter. His devoted assistant Louise (Alida Valli) drives into Paris, and lures students who

From Franju *by Raymond Durgnat (London: November Books, 1968), pp. 78–86. Reprinted by permission of the publisher.*

resemble Christiane to Genessier's home; there he attempts, vainly, to graft their faces on to hers. At last his own face is torn off by the dogs on which he intended to perform experiments, and his daughter, still faceless, wanders off into the night. The doves which, for Franju, suggest madness, hover round her head, as if their fluttering were her shattered, freed thoughts.

"When I shot *Les Yeux sans Visage* I was told: 'No sacrilege because of the Spanish market, no nudes because of the Italian market, no blood because of the French market and no martyrized animals because of the English market.' And I was supposed to be making a horror film!"

For all these handicaps, Franju seems to have succeeded only too well. The French have always admired the English penchant for horror stories, and imagined that the land of Mary Shelley, Bram Stoker, Jack the Ripper and Terence Fisher would appreciate an artistically made horror film. Alas, when it was presented in the Film Festival at Edinburgh (home of body-snatchers), seven people fainted, and public and press were outraged. Franju didn't improve matters by saying that now he knew why Scotsmen wore skirts.

In England, *Les Yeux sans Visage* was greeted with a unanimously shocked, or contemptuous, press. Critics were already disturbed by the Hammer horrors; and here was a horror film which really hurt. Almost the only reviewer in a national daily to give it a good review very nearly lost her job as a result—it's very dangerous not to conform in the world of English culture. The critics disagreed as to whether it was actually too horrible to bear, or whether it incompetently failed to horrify, or whether it incompetently failed in every respect except horrifying. (Needless to say, *Sight and Sound* bayed its utter scorn.) However, the film's reputation was rapidly redeemed, partly by the younger critics (notably Ian Cameron), partly by the slowly percolating influence of the French magazines, and partly by the retrospective prestige of Franju's more obviously respectable films, including *La Tête contre les Murs*, which wasn't imported until after *Les Yeux sans Visage*.

That the storyline contains unoriginal ingredients can't be denied; here is the mad surgeon, the secret operating-theater, the hounds. But a storyline, in itself, is hardly more significant than the storyline of a painting. In itself, it is a shell, which can be filled with rotten meat, or with pearls beyond price. The disparity between story and film can be suggested by indicating some stages which often intervene. After establishment of the storyline (or scenario) comes the masterscene script (the film divided into scene-settings and written out as a play), the shooting script or *découpage* (the shot-by-shot storyboard), revisions suggested by the director (if he didn't intervene earlier) to suit his style, and then the actual filming, which is a synthesis of contributions by scripts, director, actors, and other artists, including the most unreliably brilliant of them all, chance. A director can utterly transform a film by his control over the last two stages, and if, as in Franju's case, he also controls the *découpage*, many a trite story can be completely exsanguinated and filled with new blood. At this stage in the rapid evolution of film criticism, it can't be repeated too often that visual content in a film is just as important as visual content in a painting. Literary content corresponds to the general outlines of a painting's composition, that is, to the cartoon. Some of the meaning lies here, but rather more lies in that network of significant details which we immediately recognize as a painter's style, i.e., vision, i.e. meaning, i.e., content.

This doesn't mean that there is any need to apologize for, or explain away the horror content of *Les Yeux sans Visage*. The horror genre is as much a part of modern mythology as the Western or the detective story. It's ironical that our mythology springs either from religion or from pulp pops. The mad scientist, like the gunslinger, is a figure in our pulp pantheon. As valuable an analysis of our society's stresses and strains could and no doubt will be written in terms of these contemporary archetypes as in terms of high culture artworks. In his sensitive acceptance of the *infra dig*, Franju is heir to Apollinaire, to Cocteau and Breton, who had spotted the poetry of Arizona Bill, of Mack Sennett and Fantomas two world wars before Anglo-Saxon *littérateurs* had even begun worrying about pop culture, let alone attempting to understand it. Franju hasn't the least intention of diluting the story's pulp shocks, nor even of sublimating them. Poetic, like religious, myth has every right to concern itself with the pounding of blood and the rumbling of thunder, with indelicate sensations indelicately rendered; its finesse lies in the grafting on such libidinous roots of the more delicate stems of feeling.

Thus the cliché aspects of the story can be transformed into poetry by the styles which bathe and impregnate them. In the opening sequence, the branches along a country road are spectrally illumined by car headlights, and seem to perform an eerie dance, emphasized by Maurice Jarre's waltz, as slippery as black ice. We are launched into a fantasy realm which is only the dark lining of our routine world. Photography becomes a medium in the spiritualist sense—

this world speaks to us from beyond the grave, the grave of our belief that the everyday isn't eerie. The delicate loop described by a Citroën DS as it parks, the reflection of black branches in its black metal skin, the rhythm with which scapels are placed firmly in Genessier's rubber-carapaced hand, the morgue by a Métro station near which the trains emerge like grey ramrods into listless day, cease to be "superficial" details of style, they link the mythic and the everyday.

The film's physical details are as carefully orchestrated. One scene contrasts Valli's furs with Juliette Mayniel's raincoat; later Edith Scob in her white satin housecoat contrasts with Mayniel's rough garb of white towelling. The cables of an electro-encephalogram recall the surgical clips framing a face during an operation. The dogs wear studded collars which evoke slavery, while Valli wears a velvet choker, because she is Genessier's dog. Valli in a leather coat drags a dead girl, nude in a man's mackintosh, across rough ground in such a posture that it is almost a perverse embrace: Lesbian, necrophiliac, sadistic. Valli strokes Edith Scob's hair with a reverent sensuality, and we are reminded of the Lesbians dancing together in *La Tête contre les Murs*. But Franju is not interested in the Lesbianism of Lesbians, not even the loneliness of Lesbians, so much as in a sad and sexless dislocation of being, a contact which is at once turgid and void. The loop described by Genessier's DS, seen from above, parallels the course of his pencil over a doomed girl's face, itself a disturbing parallel to the scalpel's subsequent curve along the same line.

Christiane, believed dead, lives in her snow-coloured apartment, like a soul in purgatory, amongst satins and glossy fashion magazines, with a transistor radio, and all the mirrors replaced with black panels. Flayed alive beneath her pearly mask, she murmurs through its unmoving lips into the telephone, her fiancé's name, and he hears her speaking as if double-long-distance from a satiny grave. Marienbad was a luxurious concentration camp of the soul. Christiane's secret rooms have the same resonance, and, like X and Y, she almost returns to the land of the living. Overlaid sounds are used to "enlarge" the screen—crickets whirring, the sloppy thud of a body into a family vault, the tired throb of a passing airliner. The movement of an automobile along a road takes on the quality of a strophe— Genessier's sleek black mirror of a DS glides soft as a shark, Louise trundles about in a 2CV, humble, rustic, like a barge, in fact, *le chaland qui passe. . . .*

Such details occupy the bulk of screen time, and might have weakened rather than set off the terror. Several factors ensure that they don't. First, the Boileau-Narcejac script is unconventionally, but effectively constructed. In form it anticipates *Psycho:* a first heroine visits "Hell," is killed, and a second victim nearly takes her place. If the fates of these victims provide the principal melodramatic shocks, they also, as in Hitchcock's film, allow a certain dramatic and moral complexity. When Mayniel, having been facially skinned, escapes in Genessier's house, unaware, because of the towelling round her head, and rugged as she is, of what has happened to her, we hope she will succeed because where there's escape there's hope, if only of revenge. But we hope even more desperately that she will not escape, because then she will have to face the truth. And so we're caught in a tangle of hope and counter-hope, our optimism and pessimism are equally frightening, the melodrama loses all will-she–won't-she naivety and becomes elegiac. And when the girl lies dead, her eyes stare at us, unseeing, through slits in the towelling; hers are the eyes without a face, and, now, the eyes without the eyes.

But our principal, and subtlest, identification is with neither of these outsiders, but with Christiane, on whose behalf they are to be sacrificed. Through her, we find ourselves involved in a paradoxical concern for Louise, who loves Christiane and whose love Christiane appreciates, and even for Gennessier, who at least plans a concerned paternal role. Maybe his paternalism is an aspect of his megalomania, just as Louise's canine devotion is an aspect of her selfishness, a feeling that since Genessier saved her he can do no wrong. Provoked as quietly as they are, with direct confrontation reserved for the end of the film, the conflicts take on tones of regret, of puzzled guilt, of misplaced and doomed decency, which become the film's dramatic key, and impregnate the most melodramatic moments with deeper tones.

Second, Franju's style itself constitutes a unity, linking the everyday, the atrocious, the pessimistic, the demented, the beautiful. It's no accident that our first identification, with a victim of physical violence, leads to an identification with a victim of mystification, whose one violent act springs from a reflex of compassion. Hence, though the film horrifies, Franju was right to resist its classification as a horror film. "It's an anguish film. It's a quieter mood than horror, something more subjacent, more internal, more penetrating. It's horror in homeopathic doses."

Inevitably, of course, critics who are hypochondriac about vio-

1. *The Cabinet of Dr. Caligari* (Germany, 1919). Photo courtesy
The Museum of Modern Art/Film Stills Archive.

2. *Dracula* (U.S.A., 1931). Photo courtesy Cinemabilia.

3. *Dracula.*

4. *Frankenstein* (U.S.A., 1931). Photo courtesy The Museum of Modern Art/Film Stills Archive.

5. *Freaks* (U.S.A., 1932). © 1932, Metro-Goldwyn-Mayer, Inc. Reprinted by permission of Metro-Goldwyn-Mayer, Inc.

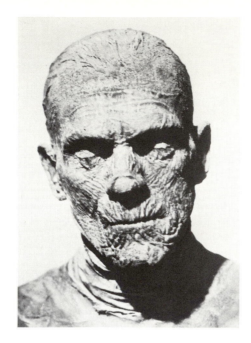

6. *The Mummy* (U.S.A., 1932).
Photo courtesy The Museum of
Modern Art/Film Stills Archive.

7. *King Kong* (U.S.A., 1933). Photo courtesy The Museum of
Modern Art/Film Stills Archive.

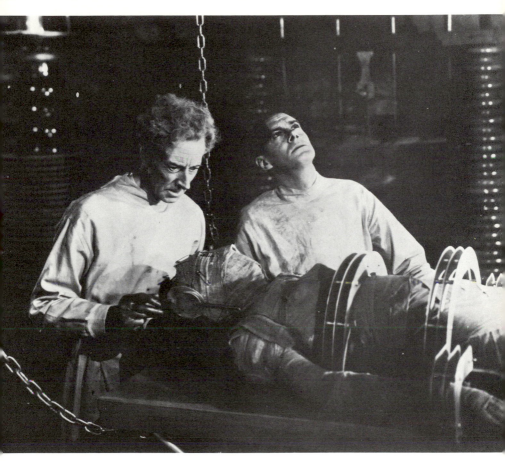

8. *The Bride of Frankenstein* (U.S.A., 1935).

9. *The Bride of Frankenstein.*

10. *House of Wax* (U.S.A., 1953). Photo courtesy The Museum of Modern Art/Film Stills Archive. Reprinted by permission of Warner Bros., Inc.

11. *The Creature from the Black Lagoon* (U.S.A., 1954). Photo courtesy The Museum of Modern Art/Film Stills Archive.

12. *Repulsion* (Great Britain, 1965). Copyright © 1965, Columbia Pictures. Reprinted by permission of Eugene Gutowski, Catherine Deneuve, and Columbia Pictures.

lence, or too coarse for poetry, or both, will respond only to the violence, which, torn out of its context, will seem either ineffective, or
only too effective, depending on the pattern of their tabus and responses. But even more disturbing than critical reactions is the urban American response described by Pauline Kael in her stimulat-
ingly demystificatory "I Lost It at the Movies":

> The theater, which holds 2646, was so crowded I had trouble
> finding a seat. Even dubbed, *Eyes without a Face* . . . is austere
> and elegant. . . . It's a symbolist attack on science and the ethics
> of medicine, and though I thought this attack as simple-minded
> in its way as the usual young poet's denunciation of war or com-
> merce, it is in some peculiar way a classic of horror . . . even
> though I thought its intellectual pretentions silly, I couldn't
> shake off the exquisite, dread images.
> But the audience seemed to be reacting to a different movie.
> They were so noisy the dialogue was inaudible; they talked until
> the screen gave promise of bloody ghastliness. Then the chatter
> subsided to rise again in noisy approval of the gory scenes. When
> a girl in the film seemed about to be mutilated, a young man
> behind me jumped up and down and shouted encouragement.
> "Somebody's going to get it," he sang out gleefully. The audience,
> which was, I'd judge, predominantly between 15 and 25, and at
> least a third feminine, was . . . pleased and excited by the most
> revolting and obsessive images. . . . But nobody seemed to care
> what the movie was about or be interested in the logic of the plot.

The psychopathic reaction has something in common with the
critical one—both are blind to anything but violence. Fortunately
neither is typical of audiences elsewhere. The present writer saw the
film three times in upper working-class family halls, where the audiences were gripped from the opening moment by the intensity of
atmosphere, and went on to a consistent identification with each victim in turn—sickened screams being provoked as Genessier lifts,
from the bloodied front of Mayniel's head, the soft plane of her ex-
pressionless, eyeless face: and later, as his pencil marks out the next
victim's face, the audience flinched as if the pencil-point were already a scalpel. If attention relaxed during one or two scenes, like
Genessier's slow walk upstairs, which remain caviare for the general,
the one detail of Franju's which, on the level of brutal efficacy, over-
reaches itself is Louise's croaking "Why . . . ?" after Christiane has
driven the scalpel into her throat. No doubt it's physically possible,

since a scalpel is a delicate instrument, no doubt the reminder of anatomical intricacy is more disturbing than the usual "bang you're dead!" stylization which renders movie violence so abstract; but the very contradiction of stabbed throat and speech is a little too startling for people to take, and needs a more analytical presentation.

One wonders, though, if Franju is really protesting against science, or medical ethics, *per se*, whether Genessier hasn't been too completely assimiliated to Baron Frankenstein. After all, his motive isn't scientific curiosity, and his conduct is hardly ethical.

Still, the overtones remain, and are reinforced by the lecture of which we catch a glimpse as the film begins: "the subject is completely exsanguinated," says the lecturer, whereupon the audience, including a Jesuit, bursts into applause. It's significant, too, that the graft Genessier attempts is currently on the border of science fact and science fiction. Plastic surgeons still have to take the new skin from another part of the patient's body, because, except in the case of identical twins, "foreign" skin mobilizes the home antibodies which attack it. Franju explained: "The hostile antibodies could be destroyed by X-ray bombardment, except that the dose needed is so massive that it would kill the patient as well. The Yugoslavs have developed a bonemarrow graft, but the face is something else again." It is possible that we might one day soon have facebanks as well as blood banks and eyebanks, or even standardized faces which the body and mind would slowly remould and reinterpret? Genessier's innovations belong to the order of disturbing scientific possibilities, like immortality by deep freeze, and so do carry a Frankensteinian overtone, of sorts.

Obviously, though, Franju isn't indicting scientific hubris in the face of any divine or natural order. It is Genessier's will to power which brought about the road accident, which so distorts his love of his daughter, and which reduces other girls to abstractions. However pure and benevolent science may be, there is certainly a scientific callousness just as there is a militaristic, a moralistic, an ideological, or any other sort of callousness. We don't need to argue a case from recondite theories about surgery only being sublimated sadism to begin with. We've all known of doctors, midwives or nurses, who don't bother with anaesthetics even though the patient is screaming, or who, in various subtle ways, use the doctor-patient situation to gratify their sadism; we have all been treated as things by doctors, who look at our disease as if we weren't there. Again, it's an open secret that many of the regulations concerning the vivisection of animals are, even in the land of the R.S.P.C.A., honoured more in the breach than in the observance. Indeed there's an eerie echo of Franju themes in a recent anti-vivisectionist advertisement, showing a photograph of a dog on to whose neck a second (dying?) head had been grafted. The photograph, revolting enough in itself, especially since the second head is from a dog of a totally different breed, becomes even more upsetting if, following Franju's practice of identifying with the victim, one asks oneself: how bewildered is the second head?

One's impression that Franju's quarry is not science *per se,* but a certain use of science, is reinforced by the other aspect of Genessier's crimes. A clue is afforded by Louise's all-but posthumous *"Pourquoi . . . ?"* to Christiane, implying: "I helped you, why stab me?" She can't understand, because she can't understand humanity, only loyalty. Genessier's callousness derives from a similar attachment, a sort of vicarious egoism, which, ineradicable in human nature anyway, derives a special resonance from the film's French context. For in a country whose bourgeoisie isn't so far removed from the peasantry, with its close, secretive family spirit, the cult of the family has a political connotation which it doesn't possess in England. The cult was a prop of Pétainist politics (as against the Resistance), and has long figured in all right-wing programs for Moral Rebirth; it links strong puritanical overtones with conservative politics, being opposed to the collectivist ideology of the left. Ravaged by Genessier's familial egoism, Christiane can oppose to it, finally, only her sense of obligation to utter strangers, a sense of indiscriminate solidarity which here becomes a left-wing attitude. Franju doesn't show us Christiane's faceless face at the end, but I believe that as she walks into the night air, freeing the dogs and the doves from her father's cages, the ghostly face hovering over her scarred tissue is the most beautiful face in the world. She is mad, but her madness is an absolute, an impossible assent to freedom, to tenderness and powerless mercy. As the mad were thought to be, she has become divine.

In this affinity of angels and animals, of those above and below the routines of rationalist calculation, the film evokes a kind of moral metaphysic and acquires a theological ring. Dr. Genessier ("Genesis") is God, who insisted on "ruling the road"—Christian orthodoxy sees pride vis-à-vis God as the original sin, but an anti-Christian metaphysic might well ascribe the megalomania to God. His daughter, Christiane ("Christian") is his creature—a female Adam, a virginal Eve. But as Genessier doesn't rule the road, she has to suffer to redeem his pride, so she's also a female Christ (orthodoxy describes Christ as the second Adam). Louise is Genessier's Holy Christ, a dark angel selecting sacrifices. And in this black, inverted theology, it's not the Son of God who is crucified for man, but woman who is flayed alive to atone for God's mad pride.

These interpretations aren't offered in the belief that allegorizing makes a film seem profounder than it is; it doesn't. But a profound meaning is held, as it were, in suspension by the intensity with which Franju's style extends a melodramatic idea into a mythological malaise.

The New American Gothic
STEPHEN FARBER

❖❖❖

"American movies have never been worse," Pauline Kael wrote recently. Her remark seems like the final sellout. Fortunately, Miss Kael only partly believes it—unlike most of our serious critics, she continues to see and review American movies. And the slump Miss Kael sees is more universal than she suggests. Where *are* the great films today? *Juliet of the Spirits, Dr. Zhivago, Red Desert, The Soft Skin* are all, in important ways, disappointing recent works from artists who have achieved masterpieces since 1960. Bright young talents fizzle. In *The Knack* and *Help!* Richard Lester breaks the exhilarating promise he made in *A Hard Day's Night*. Everywhere, it's a discouraging pattern.

The future of the American film, meanwhile, is intriguing, and it is unfortunate that almost the only energetic defenders of American movies are the *auteur* critics: in a recent *Cahiers du Cinéma* most of the contributors included *The Sandpiper* (not even low camp, by any stretch of the imagination) as one of the Ten Best of 1965. Academy Award voters are more insightful. And

From Film Quarterly 20, No. 1 (Fall 1966): 22–27. Copyright © 1966 by the Regents of the University of California. Reprinted by permission of the Regents and the author.

yet, frustratingly, *auteur* criticism alone reminds us that there are many talented film makers, above ground, in this country. American film talent has always been strained by commercial pressure, and the success of James Bond and *The Sound of Music* is not reducing the pressure. But the best American movies, in their response to that pressure, exercise a peculiar cinematic fascination. Most of the few interesting American movies of the past year or so have in common what I shall call a Gothic quality: films as different as *Lilith, Hush . . . Hush Sweet Charlotte, The Collector, Bunny Lake Is Missing,* and, most curiously, *Inside Daisy Clover.*

It is difficult to define a trend still in progress, but I am using the term "Gothic" to describe arresting distortions in both mood and cinematic technique. All of these films deal, directly or indirectly, with horror, often with absolutes of Evil. The girl in *Lilith,* for example, is not dismissible as insane; she is meant to represent a particularly haunting version of the demonic temptress-destroyer. This suggestion of demonic or nightmarish menace, often in a setting of lush, ominous decay—the classic Southern mansion of *Hush . . . Hush Sweet Charlotte*—supplies a crucial thematic resonance in these Gothic films. None of the films is naturalistic in style—all of them seek to cut beneath the "realistic" surfaces of films like *The Hustler* and *Hud* and explore extremes of feeling, often in universal terms. But the technique is not symbolic in the manner of some European films; it is a very distinctive kind of baroque and self-conscious expressionism, relying on unusually over-ripe, even violent visual exaggerations and refractions. Thus films like *Charlotte* and *Bunny Lake Is Missing,* which may not seem very new in genre, achieve unexpected, trenchant insight through a desperately bizarre tone that does not belong to the conventional American thriller.

But this Gothic quality can be better approached by considering a film in which it is altogether surprising, *Inside Daisy Clover,* written by Gavin Lambert and directed by Robert Mulligan. At first glance *Daisy* is a film with an elaborate Hollywood ancestry that fits neatly into a generic mold—still another film about the making and breaking of a star, the usual Hollywood satire-drama, Natalie Wood's version of Harlow. Yet the film is insidious in a way that almost no one has noticed. Pauline Kael did notice it, but she couldn't make anything of it; she wrote recently and unsympathetically that the film is "full of lurking evil that seems to be unrelated to anything . . . an inside Hollywood movie with a Gothic atmosphere."

A plot summary would suggest only typical slick, melodramatic stuff—sex, ambition, Lonely Girl, with a touch of nostalgia. But there is a curious sinister distortion in *Daisy's* visual temper that complicates the plot summary. Again and again Mulligan composes bizarre shots of Christopher Plummer in black, lighting and oblique camera angle designed to discompose us. Black limousines—whether arriving for a Christmas eve celebration or a wedding—lumber menacingly across the screen like implacable monsters. Mulligan exaggerates shadows, uses large spaces for startling asymmetrical perspectives, groups his figures in weirdly irregular patterns, cleverly manipulates costumes and settings to reinforce the trace of grotesqueness that hovers around the film's edges. On the night of her introduction Daisy sits in one corner of a long, narrow palatial chamber, dressed in a simple white frock; the satanic producer and his wife, in flowing black, approach her from the hallway—the incongruities provided by empty spaces, fantastic setting, color contrasts create a poignant sense of frustrated human relationships. Mulligan's visual patterns persistently suggest the film's theme of disconnection and disruption. We literally *see* the disconnections, in a technique not unlike Antonioni's.

The resetting of Lambert's novel in the Hollywood of the 1930s is not a sentimental evasion; the stylization possible in a period piece is absolutely necessary to the film's peculiar expressionism. Without the visual rhythms animated by archaic Rolls Royces and rococo gowns, the film's meaning would be blurred. Mulligan constructs a complicated world, in which a veneer of surface elegance covers a vicious waste land, Gothic visual mannerisms gradually, dramatically guiding us to recognize that what seems a palace hides a sepulchre, governed by a ghoulish "prince of darkness."

The evaluative process is more complicated than this suggests. Plummer's producer is deliberately described as a black prince because he is a highly sophisticated villain, both more sympathetic and more frightful than the usual version of the materialist-destroyer. His awareness of others is acute and delicate, and his emotional repertory is alarmingly various. In his "big" scene, after the failure of Daisy's marriage, he gently chides her for missing the cynical point of Movieland's illusion; with astonishing finesse he simultaneously comforts her, needles her, seduces her—to guarantee his investment.

Finally, that is, Plummer's world is a ruthless one, but it is a labyrinth of confusing appearances to the uninitiated: what looks like a lovely country estate is, in fact, the mental institution where Daisy's mother is hidden away and stifled; the glamorous idol Daisy marries turns out to be a homosexual. Mulligan's funereal mood, with its unsettling hints of Evil, warns us to test the appearances. And the test is tricky; consider, for example, the handling of the musical numbers. For Daisy's first audition Mulligan opens with a stunning long shot, the wide screen saturated with ominous black cameras, lighting equipment, technicians entranced for some ghastly ritual. Beyond the mass of black, in a corner, is a patch of color; slowly the camera moves in on the color, revealing it to be a particularly artificial stage set on which Daisy, in ridiculous gamin costume, has been asked to perform. But Daisy takes the set seriously. More than that, she transforms it. As she sings, against the network of shadowy equipment, surveyed by the producer's cortege, a group of dead souls mesmerized by the light, Daisy, even in tinsel, offers a poignant possibility of life in the midst of death. Her warmth, her innocence lighten the gloom and control the technology. But later, when we see the same number gussied up in the film within the film, it has been thoroughly drained of life by hideously clever camera trickery. The machine has efficiently destroyed Daisy's struggling humanity.

Daisy moves in a graveyard procession that can sterilize all it touches, yet values and sympathies do remain, desperately disguised —for a moment, in a catatonic picnic on the floor of a mental ward. One of the most tender scenes in the film occurs when the dashing homosexual whom Daisy loves finds her on the set of her new movie, in heavy clown make-up, and gently wipes her face clean. At her most garish, even in a circus, we can recognize in Daisy a touching image of possibilities of affection.

This recognition, not quite smothered by the world of ruined beauty that is crystallized for us in striking visual disconnections, prepares for the film's imaginative climax. Daisy, at seventeen, is divorced, her mother is dead, and the cruelty of the success game she has agreed to play is growing painfully clear. One morning she reports for work, enters a dubbing booth to re-record the sound for a scene she has just filmed. She must watch her image on the screen and synchronize the words she sings with the lip movements of the giant mouth before her. At first it seems easy enough, but the sound of the timing bell, of her own voice, the sight of her machine-polished self strutting on screen become more and more oppressive until Daisy goes hysterical. The scene is an ingenious cinematic representation of the disparity between public and private self, between the surface glitter of a star and the muted sensitivity of the girl buried beneath the rouge. Mulligan works the scene skillfully so that what might have been ordinary sounds and sights become grotesque and monstrous to us. As Daisy becomes distraught, Mulligan moves his camera outside her recording booth; we observe both the real Daisy and the screen Daisy from an imposed distance, and the juxtaposition of the two is made more eerie and disturbing by ominous silence, blasted finally and only momentarily by Daisy's terrified shriek as the door of her recording booth is opened and closed. This is truly a scene of horror, but also of insight—we see not only Daisy's recognition of her own separateness from the image she has been forced to project, but, by extension, our isolation from the impenetrable inner life of another, and, perhaps, from our own suppressed terrors at the travesty of our public lives. The scene conveys an expressive, summary vision of dislocation, and finally, of perverted but untouchable power.

What gives *Inside Daisy Clover* its flavor is the devious, strangely fantastic way in which it works. Mulligan's technique for portraying the integrity and isolation of self is singularly elaborate, almost overly ingenious, and therefore bizarre. Appearance and reality, mask and feeling are not simply separated, they are painfully wrenched apart. The Gothic method—the visual distortions, the near-frantic inventiveness—is the film's interest, for in its method is a madness that suggests concern. I mentioned Antonioni earlier, and it is true that Mulligan's images of disconnection are not unrelated to those of *Red Desert*. But to tentatively suggest such a comparison is to be reminded of the more pertinent differences. *Red Desert*, obviously, is without the Gothicism, the sinister and baroque touches of *Inside Daisy Clover*. If Antonioni is an expressionistic filmmaker, Robert Mulligan, in *Daisy Clover*, is expressionistic with a vengeance. It is as if the Antonioni images had been given a perverse twist; and it seems that only through such a perverse twist can a serious and original American film be produced.

As Daisy's inner self must be violently torn from her masked image, so in all recent American Gothic films piercing insight must be torn from the mask of generic convention. Otto Preminger's *Bunny Lake Is Missing*, about the disappearance of a little girl, begins as another slick London atmosphere thriller, but in its final scenes turns unexpectedly to a graphic exploration of subliminal and primitive feelings. In these scenes Carol Lynley, searching for her

child, finally finds her in the hands of her psychotic brother. He and
the child's mother enter a nerve-wracking struggle for little Bunny,
expressed in terms of a childhood game they deliriously revive. The
film's visual quality changes as it nears its conclusion—instead of
the sharp composition and neat cutting of the early scenes, the scenes
in the doll-maker's shop, in the hospital, the final confrontation in
a hide and seek game, are intensely overwrought, hysterical.

Through the visual extravagance and the nervous editing Preminger evokes a harrowing childish nightmare to suggest the child im-
perfectly submerged in the two adult antagonists. The undigested
Freudianism implicit in the quasi-incestuous encounter of brother
and sister is hardly annoying; for visual hyperbole cogently renders
the irrational but gripping fear of the perverted child latent in the
man. No other interpretation accounts for Preminger's shrewd decision to make the little girl completely passive in the scene in which
her life is at stake. Her childish terrors have been appropriated, as
it were, by her mother and uncle—a forceful external representation
of the feelings that Preminger means to suggest. Similarly effective
are the shots of the mother, who is sane, running from window to
window and pressing her face against the glass as she tries to see what
her brother is doing. Considered as realistic detail, these shots would
be absurd; as an image of the mother's chilled bewilderment at the
buried child within her psyche, they are vivid and evocative. The
nightmare of an adult's unwieldy, repressed childhood is an unusual
area for any film to explore. It is explored effectively here, in what
might have been conventional psychotic melodrama, through the
atmospheric and stylistic excesses peculiar to Gothic cinema.

Gothic cinema also provides rare moments of recognition in *Hush
. . . Hush Sweet Charlotte,* another film which would seem constricted by its genre, the Bette Davis monster movie. The best moments in *Charlotte* dramatize the close relationship of horror and
melancholy, the astonishing fact of emotional susceptibilities that
persist in the face of the most violent shocks. In an early scene, for
example, right after the brutal cleaver murder of Charlotte's lover,
a trembling Charlotte enters the ballroom, her dress swabbed in
blood, as her father slowly, caressingly approaches her; it is an in-
delible moment of macabre beauty, that flows like quicksilver from
the grotesque to the delicately poignant. Later, in a sequence of
equally powerful emotional mobility, Charlotte searches for her
dead lover in a fragrant, lingering slow-motion daydream, concludes
by shooting him with her corsage, and realizes that a real man lies

dead in the doorway of the room. To say that director Robert Aldrich is capitalizing on neurosis is probably true, but it is not entirely relevant to our experience in watching such a sequence. The film cannot be dismissed as simply sick or sensational, for its point, intentionally or intuitively rendered, is the surprising survival of vital emotion in a sick world. *Charlotte,* like other Gothic films, succeeds in apprehending, amidst the deathly flush that is its norm, a twisted, enduring humanity.

Robert Rossen's *Lilith* is a Gothic fairy tale instead of a Gothic melodrama, but again the film seeks to present to us a nightmare world—in this case a mental institution—and bring us to understand that the nightmare contains a bewitching dream of life. *Lilith* is about the beauty and destructiveness of madness, more specifically about the love of a sanitorium orderly for a gifted patient, and it aims at evoking a luxuriant but fragile lyricism that will both enchant and suggest its own qualification. Horror is always close to the film's surface, but the Gothic quality here is of a rather special nature—a richly decadent but hypnotic visual lavishness that will beguile and thus bewilder the eye, warping any clearly rational perspective.

Rossen's object is not exploitation, it is imaginative sympathy for his hero's seduction, and baroque lyric effects—composed with water and light and music—are the filmic equivalent of that sympathy. In the carnival scene that is the film's turning-point, we see that the "real"—brassy bands, chivalric games, a child selling ice—is outlandish, elusive, unreal; and the hero riding off into the woods with his princess, his sexual initiation into her magical world, are as poignant and alluring experiences as they are potentially shattering. The distorting mirror in all of these films is an illuminating one.

Whether Gothic cinema represents the death agonies or the awakening of the American film is not yet clear. Gothicism has long accounted for one strain of interesting American movies, from *Citizen Kane* to *Sunset Boulevard* to *Night of the Hunter;* exaggeration and distortion served Welles, Wilder, Agee as visual embodiment of the contorted quality of the American experience they wanted to explore. New Gothic perpetuates this characteristic vision of monstrous American blemishes and tantalizing correspondent connections of value and perversion; but the increasingly feverish quality of these recent films indicates the desperation of contemporary American cinema. In *The Manchurian Candidate,* perhaps the first in the current trend, Frankenheimer's best moments were Gothic in style—a scene like the hyperbolic press conference for the rightwing senator reminded audiences and moviemakers alike that only through freakish exaggeration could the nightmare of the American experience be realistically rendered. In addition, the film's unsettling mixture of comic-romantic-melodramatic provided a crucial jar to realism and strict generic definitions.

This formal challenge offered by the new Gothic should not be underestimated. If Gothic is appearing more frantically and in stranger places, this probably has something to do with the disappearance of the genre film in this country. Everything is spoof today, spoof Western, spoof thriller, spoof nostalgia, spoof of spoof. The genres that are thriving are lower than ever—the Joe Levine carpetbagger movie, or, worse still, the singing goofy nun movie. Gothic expressionism represents the need for surprise, the wild search by our talented movie makers for a valid film art.

The search is a treacherous one; without a firm sense of control, Gothic cinema can turn easily into striving for effect. Much of *Inside Daisy Clover* is remarkably fresh moviemaking, but some of it is fatuous trickiness. The kooky, absurdist scenes between Daisy and her mother or the laborious black comic anticlimax in which she attempts suicide by resting her head in the gas oven are nothing more than flat attempts at Something Different. Nor can sophisticated visual style cover the important hole at the film's center—the nervous skirting of the one-sided "love" relationship of Daisy and the homosexual actor. Similarly, as sympathetic as one would like to be to the expressive macabre-pathetic mood of *Hush . . . Hush Sweet Charlotte,* it is impossible to blink the low comedy or the cheap melodrama—or, in fact, the confusion of purpose—that pollutes Aldrich's inventiveness. The confusions in all of these films force us to ask if this exciting new Gothic may not soon settle into bigger and more modish thrills for the popcorn audience.

But there is really no alternative to this chaotic experimentation. We have no tradition of the film as serious art in this country, but then judging from the recent products of that tradition in France, Italy, England, the art film is prone to a fatigue no less boring than of the commercial film. If no American filmmaker today is producing films as important as the best work of the best European directors, it is equally true that many apparently hack American movies are much more interesting than the less successful efforts of Fellini, Bergman, or Antonioni. The American film, because it is commercial, challenges the creative filmmaker; he cannot simply keep re-making the same personal film, as, for example, Antonioni does. There is a lot of waste, to be sure, but when the American film is alive, it is genuinely imaginative and perceptive and startling in a way that the latest Bergman or Godard film is not likely to be. The tension between enervated generic convention and fresh, serious vision sought by the filmmaker is an important way of explaining the mannerist elements of these American movies; whether the serious vision will be achieved is still uncertain. It is interesting that *Inside Daisy Clover,* in its unsuccessful attempt to free its heroine from the System, ends simply and literally with an explosion. Gothic cinema is a kind of explosion, a strangely roundabout but violent struggle for freedom of expression.

MONSTER
TERROR

Beauty and the Beast
by WILLIAM TROY

At least one of our national characteristics is illustrated in the RKO-Radio production of "King Kong" which loomed over the audiences of both Radio City moviehouses last week. It is a characteristic hard to define except that it is related to that sometimes childish, sometimes magnificent passion for scale that foreigners have remarked in our building of hundred-story skyscrapers, our fondness for hyperbole in myth and popular speech, and our habit of applying superlatives to all our accomplishments. Efforts to explain it have not been very satisfactory; the result is usually a contradiction in which we are represented as a race that is at once too civilized and not civilized enough. If Herr Spengler interprets the extreme gigantism of the American mind and imagination as the sign of an inflated decadence resembling that of Alexandria and the later Roman Empire, others discover in it the simpler expression of a race still unawakened from childhood. At Radio City last week one was able to see the contradiction pretty dramatically borne out; an audience enjoying all the sensations of primitive terror and fascination within the scientifically air-cooled temple of baroque modernism that is Mr. Rockefeller's contribution to contemporary culture.

What is to be seen at work in *King Kong* is the American imagination faithfully adhering to its characteristic process of multiplication. We have had plays and pictures about monsters before, but never one in which the desired effect depended so completely on the increased dimensions of the monster. Kong is a veritable skyscraper among the apes. In his own jungle haunts he rules like a king over the rest of the animal world; and when he is taken to New York to be exhibited before a light-minded human audience he breaks through

From The Nation 136, *no. 3533 (1933): 326. Copyright* © *1933 by* The Nation.

his chromium-steel handcuffs, hurls down two or three elevated trains that get in his way, and scales the topmost heights of the Empire State building with the fragile Miss Fay Wray squirming in his hairy paw. The photographic ingenuity that was necessary to make all this seem plausible was considerable, and in places so remarkable as to advance the possibility of a filming of certain other stories depending largely on effects of scale—*Gulliver's Travels,* for example, and possibly even the *Odyssey*. But, unfortunately, it was thought necessary to mitigate some of the predominant horror by introducing a human, all-too-human, theme. "It was not the guns that got him," says one of the characters at the end, after Kong has been brought to ground by a whole squadron of battle planes. "It was Beauty killed the Beast." By having Beauty, in the person of Miss Wray, lure the great monster to his destruction, the scenario writers sought to unite two rather widely separated traditions of the popular cinema—that of the "thriller" and that of the sentimental romance. The only difficulty was that they failed to realize that such a union was possible only by straining our powers of credulity and perhaps also one or two fundamental laws of nature. For if the love that Kong felt for the heroine was sacred, it suggests a weakness that hardly fits in with his other actions; and if it was, after all, merely profane, it proposes problems to the imagination that are not the less real for being crude.

Who Killed King Kong?
by X. J. KENNEDY

The ordeal and spectacular death of King Kong, the giant ape, undoubtedly have been witnessed by more Americans than have ever seen a performance of *Hamlet, Iphigenia at Aulis,* or even *Tobacco Road.* Since RKO-Radio Pictures first released *King Kong,* a quarter-century has gone by; yet year after year, from prints that grow more rain-beaten, from sound tracks that grow more tinny, ticket-buyers by thousands still pursue Kong's luckless fight against the forces of technology, tabloid journalism, and the DAR. They see him chloroformed to sleep, see him whisked from his jungle isle to New York and placed on show, see him burst his chains to roam the city (lugging a frightened blonde), at last to plunge from the spire of the Empire State Building, machine-gunned by model airplanes.

Though Kong may die, one begins to think his legend unkillable. No clearer proof of his hold upon the popular imagination may be seen than what emerged one catastrophic week in March 1955, when New York WOR-TV programmed *Kong* for seven evenings in a row (a total of sixteen showings). Many a rival network vice-president must have scowled when surveys showed that *Kong*—the 1933 B-picture had lured away fat segments of the viewing populace from such powerful competitors as Ed Sullivan, Groucho Marx and Bishop Sheen.

But even television has failed to run *King Kong* into oblivion. Coffee-in-the-lobby cinemas still show the old hunk of hokum, with the apology that in its use of composite shots and animated models the film remains technically interesting. And no other monster in movie history has won so devoted a popular audience. None of the plodding mummies, the stultified draculas, the white-coated Lugosis with their shiny pinball-machine laboratories, none of the invisible stranglers, berscrk robots, or menaces from Mars has ever enjoyed so many resurrections.

Why does the American public refuse to let King Kong rest in peace? It is true, I'll admit, that *Kong* outdid every monster movie before or since in sheer carnage. Producers Cooper and Schoedsack crammed into it dinosaurs, headhunters, riots, aerial battles, bullets, bombs, bloodletting. Heroine Fay Wray, whose function is mainly to scream, shuts her mouth for hardly one uninterrupted minute from first reel to last. It is also true that *Kong* is larded with good healthy sadism, for those whose joy it is to see the frantic girl dangled from cliffs and harried by pterodactyls. But it seems to me that the abiding appeal of the giant ape rests on other foundations.

Kong has, first of all, the attraction of being manlike. His simian nature gives him one huge advantage over giant ants and walking vegetables in that an audience may conceivably identify with him. Kong's appeal has the quality that established the Tarzan series as American myth—for what man doesn't secretly image himself a huge hairy howler against whom no other monster has a chance? If Tarzan recalls the ape in us, then Kong may well appeal to that great-grand-daddy primordial brute from whose tribe we have all deteriorated.

Intentionally or not, the producers of *King Kong* encouraged this identification by etching the character of Kong with keen sympathy. For the ape is a figure in a tradition familiar to moviegoers: the tra-dition of the pitiable monster. We think of Lon Chaney in the role of Quasimodo, of Karloff in the original *Frankenstein*. As we watch the Frankenstein monster's fumbling and disastrous attempts to be-friend a flower-picking child, our sympathies are enlisted with the monster in his impenetrable loneliness. And so with Kong. As he roars in his chains, while barkers sell tickets to boobs who gape at him, we perhaps feel something more deep than pathos. We begin to sense something of the problem that engaged Eugene O'Neill in *The Hairy Ape*: the dilemma of a displaced animal spirit forced to live in a jungle built by machines.

King Kong, it is true, had special relevance in 1933. Landscapes of the depression are glimpsed early in the film when an impresario, seeking some desperate pretty girl to play the lead in a jungle movie, visits souplines and a Woman's Home Mission. In Fay Wray—who's been caught snitching an apple from a fruitstand—his search is ended. When he gives her a big feed and a movie contract, the girl is magic-carpeted out of the world of the National Recovery Act. And when, in the film's climax, Kong smashes the very Third Avenue landscape in which Fay had wandered hungry, audiences of 1933 may well have felt a personal satisfaction.

What is curious is that audiences of 1960 remain hooked. For in the heart of urban man, one suspects, lurks the impulse to fling a bomb. Though machines speed him to the scene of his daily grind, though IBM comptometers ("freeing the human mind from drudgery") enable him to drudge more efficiently once he arrives, there comes a moment when he wishes to turn upon his machines and kick hell out of them. He wants to hurl his combination radio-alarmclock out the bedroom window and listen to its smash. What subway commuter wouldn't love—just for once—to see the downtown express smack head-on into the uptown local? Such a wish is gratified in that memorable scene in *Kong* that opens with a wide-angle shot: interior of a railway car on the Third Avenue El. Straphangers are nodding, the literate refold their newspapers. Unknown to them, Kong has torn away a section of trestle toward which the train now speeds. The motorman spies Kong up ahead, jams on the brakes. Passengers hurtle together like so many peas in a pail. In a window of the car appear Kong's bloodshot eyes. Women shriek. Kong picks up the railway car as if it were a rat, flips it to the street and ties knots in it, or something. To any commuter the scene must appear one of the most satisfactory pieces of celluloid ever exposed.

Yet however violent his acts, Kong remains a gentleman. Remarkable is his sense of chivalry. Whenever a fresh boa constrictor threatens Fay, Kong first sees that the lady is safely parked, then manfully thrashes her attacker. (And she, the ingrate, runs away every time his back is turned.) Atop the Empire State Building, ignoring his pursuers, Kong places Fay on a ledge as tenderly as if she were a dozen eggs. He fondles her, then turns to face the Army Air Force. And Kong is perhaps the most disinterested lover since Cyrano: his attentions to the lady are utterly without hope of reward. After all, between a five foot blonde and a fifty-foot ape, love can hardly be more than an intellectual flirtation. In his simian way King Kong is the hopelessly yearning lover of Petrarchan convention. His forced exit from his jungle, in chains, results directly from his single-minded pursuit of Fay. He smashes a Broadway theater when the notion enters his dull brain that the flashbulbs of photographers somehow endanger the lady. His perilous shinnying up a skyscraper to pluck Fay from her boudoir is an act of the kindliest of hearts.

He's impossible to discourage even though the love of his life can't lay eyes on him without shrieking murder.

The tragedy of King Kong, then, is to be the beast who at the end of the fable fails to turn into the handsome prince. This is the conviction that the scriptwriters would leave with us in the film's closing line. As Kong's corpse lies blocking traffic in the street, the entrepreneur who brought Kong to New York turns to the assembled reporters and proclaims, "That's your story, boys—it was Beauty killed the Beast!" But greater forces than those of the screaming Lady have combined to lay Kong low, if you ask me. Kong lives for a time as one of those persecuted near-animal souls bewildered in the middle of an industrial order, whose simple desires are thwarted at every turn. He climbs the Empire State Building because in all New York it's the closest thing he can find to the clifftop of his jungle isle. He dies, a pitiful dolt, and the army brass and publicity-men cackle over him. His death is the only possible outcome to as neat a tragic dilemma as you can ask for. The machine-guns do him in while the manicured human hero (a nice clean Dartmouth boy) carries away Kong's sweetheart to the altar. O, the misery of it all. There's far more truth about upper-middle-class American life in *King Kong* than in the last seven dozen novels of John P. Marquand.

A Negro friend from Atlanta tells me that in movie houses in colored neighborhoods throughout the South, *Kong* does a constant business. They show the thing in Atlanta at least every year, presumably to the same audiences. Perhaps this popularity may simply be due to the fact that *Kong* is one of the most watchable movies ever constructed, but I wonder whether Negro audiences may not find some archetypical appeal in this serio-comic tale of a huge black powerful free spirit whom all the hardworking white policemen are out to kill.

Every day in the week on a screen somewhere in the world, King Kong relives his agony. Again and again he expires on the Empire State Building, as audiences of the devout assist his sacrifice. We watch him die, and by extension kill the ape within our bones, but these little deaths of ours occur in prosaic surroundings. We do not die on a tower, New York before our feet, nor do we give our lives to smash a few flying machines. It is not for us to bring to a momentary standstill the civilization in which we move. King Kong does this for us. And so we kill him again and again, in much-spliced celluloid, while the ape in us expires from day to day, obscure, in desperation.

A King in New York
by CLAUDE OLLIER

In 1925, the captive brontosaurus hauled back from the jungle of *The Lost World* to London to be exhibited as a circus attraction breaks his chains, plays havoc with a number of objects around Piccadilly, then is engaged in combat on the famous bridge, until he stumbles and, sliding down the whole length of the structure, causes it to collapse under his weight. Six years later, Willis O'Brien, creator of the designs and models which were the basis for these special effects, was engaged by Merian Cooper (the coproducer with Ernest Beaumont Schoedsack of such adventure films as *Grass, Chang, The Four Feathers, Rango* and the future producer of the most notable films of John Ford) to contrive a series of tableaux illustrating the possibilities of a film project the action of which was to be built round a giant gorilla. Assisted by Mario Larringa and Byron L. Crabbe, O'Brien executed a dozen designs which served to crystallize the ideas of the promoter.

The entire first design represented King Kong on top of the Empire State Building: he holds the woman in his hand as the planes rake him with machine gun fire. The second design shows King Kong in the jungle shaking a tree in order to tumble some sailors out of its branches. And in the third, Kong is seen facing the sun and beating his breast as the woman this time lies at his feet. There were twelve designs in all, eleven of which were actually reproduced during the shooting and faithfully brought to life . . . [Interview with Merian C. Cooper in *Midi-Minuit Fantastique,* No. 6 (June, 1963), p. 40].

From Cahiers du Cinéma, *nos. 166–67 (May–June 1965): 65–72. Copyright © 1965 by Les Éditions de l'Étoile. English translation by Roy Huss and T. J. Ross copyright © 1972 by Roy Huss and T. J. Ross. Used by permission of Grove Press, Inc.*

It would be most instructive to know in what order scenarists James Creelman and Ruth Rose (in private life Mrs. Schoedsack), having in mind the film's ultimate point of action, developed its other episodes. Did they invent the last sequences entirely in reverse order so that the outcome, at least for them, would not be a surprise? It is precisely in this way that the most solid fictions are sometimes achieved; for the author who begins with the end of his story, developing his plot line as it were in reverse, is obliged under penalty of death to discover absolutely ineluctable lines of causality.

It may be, however, that Creelman and Ruth Rose proceeded in the way it is ordinarily supposed that scriptwriters work, which is to say in a forward movement like that of the hands of a watch rather than as retracers of a course of time as yet unrecorded. In either case, all the leading motifs of the film are to be found in O'Brien's initial inspiration, which provides indeed a veritable blueprint for the plot: Beauty, a privileged value, protected from a social milieu that is itself in distress, becomes witness to a mortal combat between the forces of mechanized civilization and the Gorilla-God of primitive nature. (Nor is it accidental that she should appear to be less terrified in these harrowing climactic moments than she is at her story's "beginning," a matter not to be explained simply on the basis that fear tends to work itself out through its physiological expression.) As to the Beast—it is shown to be more concerned, in its pathetic fury, with defending Beauty against the flying machines than itself: as it drops its guard for a moment to assure itself of its protegé's safety, it is machine-gunned in the back by the Spads of the rash U.S.R.A.F.

Thematically, the film stresses the conjunction between the stupefying power of theatrical spectacle and the stock market activity bound up with it, and the way this in turn inexorably leads to a catastrophic depletion and disorder—disasters of a kind which seem nonetheless to have been unconsciously wished for by the populace. Thus a main influence contributing to the chaos is the extravagant role played by a public entranced by the star system: the "prehistoric" lead promoted to the role of star is revealed to be a god of love and, for that reason, of destruction. Finally, and most importantly, the presence of the monster atop the skyscraper drives home the parallel between the worlds of the jungle island and the modern metropolis.

The scenario of *King Kong,* which culminates in so grandiose an image, is made up of ingredients out of three well-tried plots: *The*

Sorcerer's Apprentice, Beauty and the Beast, and *The Lost World.*
These ingredients are combined in a single work which possesses an
uncommon richness of implication. It is shocking therefore to find
the most favorably disposed among its earliest reviewers applying
to this masterpiece of symmetry the epithet "infantile" (even granted
that the first reel of the film—since fortunately restored—was missing when the film was first shown in France, toward the end of 1933).
For the appeal of *King Kong* after all depends on a plastic beauty
unequalled in its genre; on the remarkable quality of its dreamlike
configurations; and on a power of erotic suggestion compelling
enough to make generations of high school kids amorous of the big
monkey—a creature at once scarifying and cosily protective.

It will be worth pausing, then, for a closer look at the action of
this fable. How does it work? Consider first the prime mover of the
action: a producer-author (who is in the bargain a capitalist, a director of production, a scenarist, a cameraman, and a set designer!)
sets sail for the umpteenth time for an unexplored region where he
hopes to film another in the string of exotic spectaculars for which
he is renowned. And the initial steps of his project are shrouded in
secrecy, including all specific details concerning the voyage; it is all
very much indeed "a staging in the abyss." Not only are we faced
with the unpredictable—only partly foreseeable—events which lie
ahead when the shooting of the film actually takes place, but also
with a most parsimonious yielding of information in the scenario
of the film *we* are seeing. There is, to be sure, one clear motive for
these early precautions: if the crew members had the slightest hint
of what awaited them at journey's end, nothing would induce them
to board ship. The guarded disclosures, offered piecemeal, also serve
to reinforce the tone in general of an adventure movie; at the same
time the slow, teasing unravelling of points of information allows
for the dramatic underscoring of certain main themes and the suggestion by delicious foreshadowings of the real import of the drama
to come. If, for example, the film's daredevil hero, Carl Denham
(played by Robert Armstrong), is concerned for the first time in his
career with engaging a leading woman for one of his productions, it
is because both the critics and the public have joined in insisting
that he now mix sex with his usual brand of exoticism. His present
enterprise then is in large measure a response to a collective wish.
Nor is it merely a matter of chance that brings Denham ashore to
pick out his future star from among the anonymous crowd on the
streets; in the course of his seemingly aimless stroll, his attention is

drawn by the outcry of a woman being shoved about (as she is held in the grip of a fruit vendor who had caught her trying to snitch an apple from his stand). Her cry of anguish echoes with the mystery of an ambiguous expectation, a mystery whose force will not be dissipated until the arrival of the film company at their island destination. Although Denham has a scenario in mind for his island project, his method of working is one we would now find thoroughly up-to-date as he seeks to bring within the—of necessity—tentative framework of his scenario three uncertain and "unstable" elements: an unexplored terrain inhabited by a primitive populace, a young American woman, and a legendary creature which is neither man nor beast and in its essence quasi-divine. Inevitably, improvisation will be the rule. In preparation for the monstrous psychodrama he envisages in the forthcoming encounter between prehistory and the industrial age, Denham devotes the leisure hours of their ocean voyage to rehearsing his Beauty: decking her out in costumes especially designed for her role, coaching her in the arts of mime and devising exercises for her voice in the upper register to get it attuned for the most reverberative expressions of terror. In the case of the Beast, Denham will direct him as best he can, blithely backed up, when necessary, by gas grenades. Everything to do with the island conforms to a classically mythic pattern: thus, the Norwegian sailor who had turned the map over to Denham had himself never seen the fabled spot; it was from the native survivor of a shipwreck that he had heard about it. So too the Victorian style in narrating adventure stories—with its earnest tone, its leisurely pace, and its naive and archaic flavor—is scrupulously adhered to. The voyage is menaced by an incoming monsoon gathering speed; by a deviation off-course from the standard maritime route; by a captain increasingly ill-at-ease with a restive crew—all topped off with the dangers of heat, fog, submerged reefs. But the isle awaits—it exists—as does Kong, whose name, once uttered, strikes upon the ears of the hardened seamen like some submerged memory risen from the stormy deeps of time.

His first day's shooting on the isle surpasses all of Denham's hopes. Then, in a stunning reversal of fortune, Denham is himself overwhelmed by scenes more visually breathtaking than anything he had dared to imagine—in consequence of the natives' taking his star prisoner and in effect stealing his thunder as directors of the ensuing action! Denham regains the initiative by sheer dint of force, substituting for the film record of an exotic spectacle, which he had planned to make, the raw spectacle itself. He traps the monster and gets it on board his ship, with the plan of exhibiting it "in person" in New York, together with the heroic men who had taken it captive. Here is one of those rare instances when the real actors in an event promise to be more impressive and memorable than their pattern as traced on celluloid.

But there is another way, no less faithful to it, of looking at this fable and apprehending its meaning: we have in Denham a redoubtable businessman who—disturbed and stimulated by an economic depression of unprecedented magnitude, one which has shaken his country to its foundations—decides to mount a show which will be so enormous in scale as to exorcise, or at least overshadow by its own spectacle, widespread social anxieties. In face of the grave and unforeseen peril of the financial crisis, the authorities remain without either a coherent plan of action or the imagination to conceive any fundamental revision of the system. Leaving his country, where an anguished populace trembles before the specter of its doom, Denham journeys to an unknown and virgin terrain, where he finds a primitive people who are also exposed to a frightening menace, this one of a permanent, indeed quasi-eternal, nature. The natives, however, are capable of dealing with the threat in a manner which seems more or less to have worked, at least up to the moment of Denham's arrival in their midst. Drunk with his prospects for profit, and failing completely to recognize the local wisdom, which he treats with all the contempt of an honest white racist, Denham succeeds in record time, like the "imprudent merchant" of the fairy tale who makes too little of Beauty, not only in causing the death of several of his crew in grisly circumstances, but also in destroying the fragile equilibrium between God-Beast and man established on the island by the native witch doctors. Enraged by Denham's mindless and exploitative intervention, the majestic Beast shatters the ancient ramparts of the village and lays it waste. Nor is this enough to satisfy the marauder: obsessed with his contemptible objective, Denham mobilizes every technological resource at his disposal in order to transplant the gigantic hellbent creature to his own country, where he remains heedless of what this will cost his compatriots in life and property. Only by means of the most advanced weaponry is he able to check and—finally—destroy the monster. It is precisely in consequence of the heedless and destructive shenanigans of one of its leading citizens that the menace on the human scale which hovers over the New World is multiplied by a far more terrible menace of superhuman proportions. An enigmatic power beyond rational comprehension is now unleashed on the metropolis with a clearly punitive force: in confrontation with a mean, unjust, and degrading culture, a vengeful aspect of nature, in all its "horror" and violence, looms over the general chaos of civilization to rescue the one noble human it has encountered and to destroy whatever it sees as threatening to engulf her.

Having noted, then, some of the moral and social overtones developed through the interplay of the film's characters and its star monster, we may turn now for a closer view of the two main locales which are so deftly placed in parallel by the scenario—a scenario the "puerility" of which keeps proving most complex indeed! First, there is the domain of Kong, Skull Island, so named since it is shaped like a skull or an inverted cup: a tiny peninsula spread out at the foot of an immense mountain, Skull Island corresponds exactly to that other island, Manhattan, the tip of which juts out from the foot of giant skyscrapers. On Skull Island, a resourceful people subsist as best they can on the lowlands in proximity to the ominous cliffs, just as the denizens of the city swarm round the buildings within which all-powerful beings impassively toy with and juggle the fate of the crowd. In either sphere, we behold the bulwarks of prosperity and security giving way: on Skull Island, the shattering of the bolt on the gate of the village wall corresponds to the floodgates of the city burst open by the financial tidal wave of "the crash." The equilibrium maintained by both spheres is smashed, with the difference that the dwellers on Manhattan will find themselves facing both perils—of nature and finance—together.

We may note too that it is the white man who sounds the gong to call to the rescue those same black men whom he had just before accused of cowardice and whom he then betrays to a massacre through his own folly. Thus a maddened Kong, at loose for the first time in the village, indiscriminately attacks first one group, then another. It is true that the whites clear the isle of the dread presence of Kong, but then it is also true that Kong had served on occasion to rid this land of other giant beasts roaming its surface. After the forays of the whites, little is left the islanders in any case but to bury their dead and to seek to rebuild their gate against those truly remorseless monsters who will be returning once more to breach the gate and with whom no pact is conceivable.

Thus we behold two jungle worlds in parallel. The remarkable meshing of special effects by which the jungle of Skull Island is created—models, transparencies, articulated scaffolds, "stop action"

—becomes so powerfully suggestive that the dreamlike aura of Skull Island is transposed onto the landscape of that other, modern jungle, which is made up in great part of very real views of the American metropolis. This expansion of the fantasy through seeing one universe in terms of the other evidently constitutes the film's basic line of force. There is another law ruling each of these worlds, however, which merits note (the close study of which would provide a field day especially for stock market analysts).

Regarded purely as a marketable commodity in a capitalist society, the heroine, Ann Darrow, is virtually of no worth when we see her in the beginning as a penniless waif; as soon as Denham engages her, she takes on, in contrast, great potential value. Then when the natives of the isle offer her up to Kong, her value is further raised to the category of an object for barter. Once in the possession of Kong, she becomes an amorous cult object: another promotion. Recovered by Denham, she falls back a couple of notches in the scale of values, but her rate of exchange in consequence climbs dizzily. In repossessing her and elevating her out of the reach of his mercenary counterparts, King Kong saves his lady fair from one kind of degrading "fetishism": the anger of Kong is explained as much by the larceny of which he has been the victim as by the frivolous disrespect shown him and his costar by the theater audience. The uneven destiny of Ann is perforce closely bound with the conditions of life prevailing in her social group: it is as exemplary in its glory as in its panic; and this is precisely the meaning carried from start to finish by the piercing modulations of her scream. "Your only chance is to scream," says Denham to her on the ship. From the beginning this cry predestines her for violence; indeed the misadventures of Ann in *King Kong* prefigure those of another American heroine, one equally predestined: Melanie of Hitchcock's *The Birds*. The link between the individual and the collective fate by progressive amplification and final generalization is continuously established in the two films. Melanie brings about the unleashed fury of the birds as Ann does that of the gorilla. After her, the neighborhood group, then society in the aggregate, then the nation as a whole, successively become prey to devastation. The famous "too lengthy" first part of *The Birds* matches exactly the first half of *King Kong,* during which nothing supernatural occurs, when the action includes no more than subterranean flickers of apprehension concerning the "favored" individual, these hints and intimations later communicating themselves rapidly to larger and larger social units. And one matter which in *The Birds* is treated extensively (Melanie's past efforts at social advancement) is in *King Kong* elided and condensed in Ann's shimmering outcry: it is her signal faculty for projecting to perfection various facets of her terror by her voice alone which leads Denham to "discover" her, even as Melaine Daniels is singled out by Mitch as he notices her little "innocent" machinations.

In any case, New York is saved from destruction, and it is Denham who has the last word as he delivers a funeral oration over the body of the vanquished beast. In contrast, the concluding scene of Hitchcock's film is still dominated by the presence of thousands of threatening winged creatures, seemingly in a state of truce before possible resumption of their attack. Only in prosperous times, like the America of 1963 (when *The Birds* was first shown), would such an ending heavy with uncertainty and menace be tolerated; the America of 1931, however, when *King Kong* began taking shape, was bound to insist on a standard "happy ending." (It is precisely in an era of the fatted calf such as the sixties that a "no limits" freedom of artistic expression is most readily allowed: 1963, for example, is also the year of *Dr. Strangelove,* a film in which New York is wiped out at the stroke of a presidential pen.)

But to return to Ann's nightmare experience (Fay Wray, who plays Ann, will also be especially remembered for her portrayal of Mitzi, the enticing and beleaguered beauty of Erich von Stroheim's *The Wedding March*). Nearly all the episodes during which our heroine changes masters take place at night. With a glance that increasingly mingles hints of lasciviousness with astonishment and terror, Ann endures in succession being virtually shanghaied by Denham, kidnapped by the natives, taken possession of by Kong on the sacrificial altar, and later repossessed by the creature in the high chamber of the palace (in a sequence which anticipates the inevitable finale when Kong climbs the skyscraper). A main exception: when the first mate Driscoll (Bruce Cabot) takes Ann and races off with her while Kong is occupied in his fight with the pterodactyl (or is it pterandodon?). At this point in the action there occur two vertically steep drops into the abyss—the sort of thing the cinema has found to be its most apt means for registering that kind of abrupt and incomplete resolution of tensions—and consequent swooning sensation—which marks the culmination of a nightmare. Thus we see Ann and Driscoll make their descent down a providential vine and take a dizzying fall into the waters incredibly far below. Dissolutions and recrystallizations of terror are by this exciting means woven together in a series of actions which conclude as Ann races along a sinuous path of escape, her hair flying free and her body at last somewhat relaxed after the convulsive tremors caused by her ordeal.

In another of the jungle sequences there is communicated one of the most hallucinatory and surreal sensations that the screen has ever given us: when she falls from on top the tree where Kong had placed her for safety, Ann witnesses a duel to the death between her guardian ape and an attacking tyrannosaurus. In this sequence the distinction maintained between the foreground where Ann is seen, helpless and appalled, and the middle distance where the monsters go through their paces, is as thin as a hairline—so that we are made to doubt our sense of a spatial demarcation between the two locations: the beasts are obviously quite near, since they keep bumping against the trunk of the overturned tree; and yet their confrontation (in medium-long shot) is enacted in a disorientingly close and "imponderable" perspective. Ann's terror stems both from the immediate proximity of the combatants (and the immense danger this puts her in) and from the weird sensation of unreality evoked by the spectacle. But if there were some basic "daylight" logic to the business, it would be shattered soon enough by the frightful glancing blows exchanged by the monsters. It is at this moment that the split between dream and reality is most flagrant: in large measure, what Ann is here witnessing is her own nightmare. Displacements of a similar kind, although less immediately evident, prevail almost continually during the scenes of combat; for example, the "too rapid" progression of the brontosaurus which, surging up out of the marsh, pursues a band of sailors across the jungle. In this instance, several effects of different origin are brought into play and combined: the breaks more or less visible in the succession of medium shots; the transition from medium-long to medium shots of Kong, with that extraordinary full face dolly-in on Kong's incensed features; and especially the jumps achieved by shooting "frame by frame." We may note, then, how even the minor flaws in the continuity of perspective or movement, far from destroying or enfeebling the credulity of the spectacle, are in accord rather with the presentation of a totally dreamlike state, a dream created by means of spatial illusion, optical displacement, and disruptions between individual shots and the overall continuity. The "doubtful" space created by the depth montages of O'Brien and the necessity of filming in fragmented time results in a visual pattern altogether of a kind with the sort of "collage" manifest in all visions of nightmare worlds—pointillistic effects of space and time, gaps, fringes, overflowings, and scenic incompatibilities, zones of vacant expanses where any suspicion of unreality is overcome in the all-engulfing eeriness. Moreover, the few "errors" in scale evident on occasion between the proportions of King Kong and those of his environment add to the compartmentalizations characteristic of dreams, in which agreements of size between objects are in constant evolution. (It is a pity that shots of Denham's companions being devoured by giant spiders at the bottom of the precipice from which the men had toppled have not been preserved in the extant version—at the wish, it would seem, of the producers themselves.)

From the purely plastic point of view, the creations of O'Brien, as fully limned on paper as created on film, are of a beauty which is strange, sumptuous, and overflowing: this jungle rich in its geographically inauthentic vegetation, inhabited by animals more legendary than scientifically prehistoric, derives directly from engravings that several centuries of tales of adventure have inspired. For example, one rediscovers in the scene of the subterranean lake the same chiaroscuro found in many a composition illustrating Jules Verne or Paul d'Ivoi. In certain compositions of rocky plateaus, the kinship with Gustave Doré is clearly evident. We know too that the tableau of Skull Island directly reproduces the celebrated "Isle of the Dead" of Arnold Boecklin. The director Fritz Lang had himself borrowed from three of Boecklin's works for the composition of two of the sequences of his epic film *Die Niebelungen*. Concerning the animation of the King of the Jungle, secrecy continues to shroud the different techniques that either successively or concomitantly went into the work. Because of the gorilla's superb posture and movement, it is hard to disabuse the spectator of the idea—which is false—that the "role" of Kong was played by a human being, so much does the character impose itself by its *élan vital*—one is tempted to say by its "humanity." Finally, on the matter of the film's cruelty, its horror runs the gamut of suffocation, devouring, strangulation, quartering. There are also bonus bits unequalled in monster films: witness the enormous paw with the claws meticulously curved crushing the body of a hapless native in the spongy mire.

King Kong, masterpiece of the fantastic film and assuredly one of the most disturbing, was made in the most audacious period in film history. No doubt its impressiveness is due in large part to the skills of an exceptional team. Yet the answer to its success does not lie there, but rather in the sources from which the team was inspired to draw. O'Brien and his collaborators renew, across the span of literature, painting, and engraving, a kinship with an abounding tradition of legends and illustrated myths. It is certainly more agreeable to explore among these materials than among the junk heaps of pseudoatomic science fiction, of which the dismal and ugly *Goldfinger* marks the nadir. A single regret perhaps: that the authors of the scenario had not faithfully pursued to the end the story that Denham had promised to shoot. Another possible happy ending would have removed the major uncertainty overshadowing the second appearance of the bestial creature, a mystery still unsolved: what expression would King Kong have assumed if, in those last shots, Ann had loved him?

Monster Films
by LAWRENCE ALLOWAY

Hammer Films, a British company that specializes in horror, have presented the Frankenstein Monster, Dracula, and now, the Mummy in color for the first time. American companies, although originating these monsters, have, for the most part, confined them to the black-and-white small screen or cell on which they first appeared, a quarter-of-a-century ago. The polish and ghoulishness of Hammer's highly successful films make them the liveliest things in current British film production. The company has, shrewdly, not risked new monsters but applied new technology to an existing teratology. *The Curse of Frankenstein* and *Dracula* were both re-makes of the famous originals, not further adventures of the known monsters. Neither of Hammer's recent productions has original stories: *The Mummy* is based on a Boris Karloff movie (1932) of the same name, and *The Man Who Could Cheat Death* is a version of Barre Lyndon's play *The Man in Half Moon Street*. This is not a lack of enterprise by the studio; it is typical of the special character of monster-making in the movies.

Monsters are long-lived. Monster films made in the early days of sound still go round the scream circuit, earning money years after their reputable competition has been forgotten. All the classics of horror have triggered off chains of sequels, so that the monsters stay among us. For instance, the original Mummy was followed, during the 1940s, by *The Mummy's Hand, The Mummy's Ghost,* and *The Mummy's Curse*; finally, even Abbott and Costello met the Mummy. The Frankenstein monster and Dracula, as well as the less important Wolfman (who has never had a feature film to himself), have all been

From Encounter 14 *(January 1960):* 70–72. *Copyright* © *1960 by* Encounter. *Reprinted by permission of the editors of* Encounter *and the author.*

through widely distributed repeat appearances. No wonder a science-fiction writer like Cyril Kornbluth wrote: "If I wanted to make some money in a hurry and didn't care how, I'd write a 'monster' story." Kornbluth's reaction tells us something about monster movies which you cannot learn from the film critics. It is twenty years since the bug-eyed-monster phase of science-fiction. Hence the confusion film (and book) reviewers make between science-fiction and monster-lore is a source of embarrassment to serious science-fiction fandom. Almost all so-called "science-fiction" films are, in fact, monster films, with their iconographical roots in Mary Shelley and Bram Stoker, not in 20th-century technology (which is the core of modern science-fiction). Hence the best name for the *genre* is, probably, Monster Films.

The monster film is inseparable from revivals, sequels, re-makes. In no other form of film-making is this degree of Byzantinism acceptable: in Westerns the motivation of the hero and of his enemies has changed. But the monster film is constant: Frankenstein is still a fanatical scientist who trespasses on God by creating life; Dracula still takes his blood from the neck, never from the bank; and Charis the Mummy lumbers around strong-arming Egyptologists under the same old age-old curse.

Monster films are written down and written off by regular film critics, with complaints that such films are repetitive, lack decent stories and, anyway, are sickening. It is true that good stories are not what you go to monster films for; story lines are usually nonchalant and discontinuous, studded with islands of horror, set-pieces, expected by the audience and flinched at (or screamed at) when they do happen. It is pointless to expect classic forms of suspense to be built up by hints and implications while the monster is delayed, as in literary ghost stories. The reasons for making and witnessing monster films is the visibility of the monster, the damage to persons and property, the suggestion of rape as the monster carries off the girl. Unlike the discreet forms of ghost story, shock, astonishment, fear, are the product of the monster parade. A spokesman for Hammer said recently that their films were intended "to have exactly the same effect on the audience as the Big Dipper. . . ." Characteristically, *The Mummy* is interesting only when the Mummy is on-camera —heaving out of the swamp, slithering into the padded cell, bursting into the library, staring red-eyed at the girl.

Movie-monsters take two forms: the man in a monster suit, stick-

ing pretty close to the human image (though not quite); and oversize
invaders from the wonders of nature (such as giant ants or spiders).
It is the human-image monsters, however, which carry the greatest
significance. They always have a statue-come-to-life gait and bearing
(the nimble Dracula excepted). The men in the make-up department
and Christopher Lee have done the Mummy very well. Its walk, stiff
after millennia of entombment, experimentally flexing its limbs as
it goes, is a brilliant extension of the original lumbering walk that
Karloff created; the dried hollowness of the bandaged body, a powerful crust, is creepily conveyed, too. It is cratered with deep and un-
bleeding gun-shot wounds and when a victim stabs at it with a spear
the weapon bursts dustily and unhindered through the torso and
out the back. It is worth noting how close the Mummy keeps to Mary
Shelley's original description of the Frankenstein monster:

> I saw how the fine form of man was degraded and wasted; I
> beheld the corruption of death succeeded to the blooming cheek
> of life; I saw how the worm inherited the wonders of the eye and
> brain.

She described, too, how the monster's "yellow skin scarcely covered
the work of muscles and arteries beneath."

The Man Who Could Cheat Death is about how a man who keeps
young by means of gland operations fails to celebrate his 105th birth-
day. There are some gruesome bits along the way, especially that
"laboratory humor" Hammer films are so good at (see *The Revenge
of Frankenstein*), but the final dissolution is the thing. Dorian Gray-
wise, the man's hair falls out in tufts; his skin creases and discolors;
his muscles collapse—yanking his features out of shape; and his
flesh decays until he is like one of those degraded figures horror
comics used to describe: "his body a mass of black rot," with "small
spongy chunks dropping away with each stiff staggering step."

Attempts to account sociologically for monster films always make
them symptoms of "a sick society." The analysts attempt to attach
peaks of monster-film production to whatever events in the political
calendar especially worry them. Thus, the first peak (1932–33) was
on "the eve of Nazi-ism"; the second peak (1943) was during the
"dark days" of World War II; and the third peak (now) is treated as
evidence in advance for "ban the bomb" people with monsters as
portents of radiation hazards. It is true that some recent monster

films have made ionizing radiation the agent of dreadful change (for example, *The Incredible Shrinking Man* and *The Amazing Colossal Man*) but, in pre-Atomic films electricity produced similar results. After all, something is needed to produce the monster, a direct curse, or an alternating current. The fact is, sociological explanations of this kind fail to recognize the historical fact that there has always been a spontaneous human taste for monsters, for the more-than or less-than-human. St. Augustine felt they had to be "allowed for" and explained them as part of God's inexplicable plan of the world.

The physical details of injury, malformation, and decay are paraded before us in monster films as in a medieval Dance of Death. What the monster-film does is play with death and disintegration, probing into the fearful territory around and below the healthy and intact human image. This is done despite the British censor who weakened the climaxes and central interest of both *The Mummy* and *The Man Who Could Cheat Death*. We are barely allowed to glimpse the Mummy shattered by a shot-gun volley, and the accelerated onslaught of disease and decay in *The Man Who Could Cheat Death* is jumpy and curtailed. As it is, Hammer Films make three versions: the longest and roughest for Japan; then a version for America (a bit shorter); and, finally, gentlest of the lot, a British version. For instance, embalming procedures in *The Mummy* are almost gone from the British version. The British censor, though lately admitting the existence of sex, continues to obstruct popular imagery of death.

The emphasis in these films is on the body as a package, which can be opened. What we find fills us with awe and horror. Death both repels and rouses, and monster films exploit the ambiguities of repulsion and curiosity. The *genre* is repetitive precisely because death and malformation have to be presented in rigid conventions, or disgust would overwhelm curiosity. These films are an imagery, both fantastic and highly conventional, of what happens to flesh, of the fate of being a body.

Society and the Monster
by JOHN D. DENNE

Monster movies are a form of social problem play in that they deal with deviance from the norm. Other types of films dealing with the problem of deviance include westerns, detective stories, comedies, etc., which not infrequently handle social, moral, psychological, political, and ethnic deviance. The monster movie, however, deals with a deviant (or deviants, forming a composite problem, or composite monster) which is easily and readily discernible by its *physical* form. Its motivations are for the most part inconsequential, as we view the monster as a problem which society faces in different ways. Science-fiction films may well be monster movies, if the monsters are central to the plots, but not all movies with a monster are monster movies, just as all films with deviant characters are not concerned with the problem of deviance as an integral part of the plot.

THREE TYPES OF MONSTER MOVIES

What might be called the *atmospheric* monster movie is one in which the environment in which the struggle takes place is that of the monster, or, more usually, that of society as distorted and changed by the monster and his forces (*The Mummy's Ghost*; *Dracula*). The *bipartite* (or bipolar) monster movie is one in which the struggle occurs between and among two distinct environments (*The Day the World Ended*; *Creature from the Black Lagoon*). The *social* monster movie is one in which society's environment remains very much intact and dominant, and the monster operates in our culture, out of his own (*Gorgo*; *Godzilla*).

The atmospheric movie generally has the monster as protagonist,

From December 9, *nos. 2–3 (1967): 180–83. Copyright* © *1967 by* December. *Reprinted by permission of Curt Johnson, publisher.*

malevolent, antisocial, and strong in the sense of moral consistency of behavior. The bipartite movie is relatively asocial in its approach, leaving the audience freer to observe more of a tactical battle, with neither side dominantly protagonistic. The social film presents the pure problem of deviance (always the antagonist) *within* society, and, usually, the ill effects of nonconformity on all concerned.

Briefly, the three types of movies can be viewed as the struggle between good and evil (atmospheric), a struggle between strong opponents (bipartite), and as a vindication of the *status quo* (social). Chronologically, the atmospheric had its heyday until the early and mid-forties; the bipartite, from then until the mid-fifties; the social, until now.

Atmospheric Monster Movies

The atmospheric monster movie reflects society's view toward evil that was characteristic of earlier film audiences. The popularity of this subgenre in the thirties reflects the acceptance by society of its antagonist as an impersonal force, able to disrupt and potentially destroy society. This has obvious implications in the relationship of society to the Great Depression. Prior generations viewed World War I and other foreign wars in much the same way—as irresistible evils. However, a considerable part of this attitude, or predisposition, can be traced to the average socioeconomic level of film audiences. Whereas drama and literature have usually been associated with society's intellectual group (which has generally upper-class values), the motion picture has appealed most to the masses. Thus, the typical feelings of the culturally deprived—that forces of evil, Fate, and the un-understandable can and do bear them down—is shown in atmospheric horror films.

The Mummy's Ghost (1944) is exemplary of this type. The simple plot concerns a living mummy reactivated (third film in the series) by an Egyptian priest in order to aid in returning a stolen mummy. Although the mummy fails, it is not society which is triumphant. The everyday world is ignored, cast aside, and crushed by the all-pervading atmosphere of Ancient Egypt and the supernatural forces which, through Fate, do not achieve their ends. Conventional weapons, heroics of the hero, authority in the form of the Bumbling Law, the invariably ineffective Mob, "clever" tricks and ruses (such as a pit for the mummy to fall into), and all of society's knowledge (the usually successful Learned Professor is strangled for his trouble) fail to affect the plot development or denouement. The hero is foiled, the heroine destroyed, and society shown to be powerless against "The Ancient Gods." This last is directly implied by an off-stage narration of the "moral" at the conclusion. The finale is a smashing crescendo of emotion, a rare orgasmic catharsis which is unique in monster films.

In *Dracula* (1931) Bela Lugosi's orchestra-hall speech, "To die . . . to really die . . . that must be wonderful," emphasizes the unworldliness of the plot's setting. Dracula, whether at home in Transylvania or visiting London, moves within his own supernatural environment and carries with him his own set of mores and values. Careful mood-setting (development of "atmosphere") is critical to the effective suspension of disbelief in this movie, as in most others of the category.

In *Ghost of Frankenstein* (1942) a succession of simple lines that world seem ludicrous out of context serve to heighten the atmosphere (in all senses). The action is limited to night scenes, dank cells, ruined castles, storms, mysterious laboratories, etc. *House of Frankenstein* (1945) veers toward a psychological probe of monsters, with no major character normal, and almost everyone with a line in the film being destroyed by the end. Here, through successive locales, the monsters carry with them their own violent environment. Rather than the bolerolike effect of the finale of *The Mummy's Ghost,* with society more and more helpless, here we have a symphonic repeated-crescendo effect which runs through three climactic codas, with no effect on the plot by society. There is no hero. Each attempt at resistance by society or its representatives is quickly suppressed.

Other notable examples of atmospheric monster movies are *Frankenstein* (1931), *The Invisible Man* (1933), *Son of Frankenstein* (1939), *Night Monster* (1942), *I Walked with a Zombie* (1943), *House of Dracula* (1945), *Face of Marble* (1946), *Curse of the Undead* (vampirism in a western setting, 1959), and *Black Sunday* (1961).

Bipartite Monster Movies

The bipartite monster film came into popularity at the end of World War II, and reached its peak in the mid-fifties. The intensity of the "cold war" feelings during that period was much greater than today. Today's world, still bipolar in political nature, is far more amenable to peaceful coexistence ideas than that of 1945–55. The bipartite horror film reflects the concern of society with the struggle for power within the bipolar world of the period.

The Day the World Ended (1956) is one of the prime examples of the bipartite monster movie, with a nearly completely asocial point of view. In this movie, an atomic war has destroyed all (or most; this is never clarified, and is immaterial) of the world (as we know it). A handful of survivors seeks refuge in an uncontaminated valley, while without, amid the swirling radioactive fog, lurk strange mutations who have adapted to their new environment.

Forays are made by both camps into that of the respective enemy; neither group can long live outside its own environment. No conclusion is drawn, for with the coming of the nonradioactive rain (which might have been radioactive) the valley is saved from imminent overcoming, but the outer environment remains. As a subplot, the leading mutant (formerly heroine's husband) keeps trying to win her back. His dying in the rain removes all presumed cause for conflict between the two sets of creatures, and happiness reigns —a standoff between equal combatants.

The Creature from the Black Lagoon (1954) was popular enough to go through several sequels. In the original film, the monster is found lurking in the stagnant primordial depths of a mysterious tropical lagoon. Society in the form of an expedition comes into the region, bringing its own technology and environmental components in the form of a small ship and all its equipage.

The monster is theorized to be a representative of a prehistoric species resulting from parallel evolution to man—that is, a representative of underwater people. His goals and aspirations are the same (in the circumstances) as, but of necessity, opposed to, man's. Here we have a basic man-nonman struggle representing our prehistoric struggle against other species.

The monster cannot survive long in the surface world above the water line; the men, not long below the surface, even with their SCUBA gear. The monster is relatively more deadly outside his element than the men are outside theirs, but each faction is superior within its own place. The victory of the men in such a situation becomes more of a victory of Society's environment over an alien one than a personal victory. The sun, light, and normalcy of the world above the water is repeatedly contrasted with the dark, unwholesome, and macabre world below. The opponents make forays, each against the other, with resultant destruction of the monster.

The sequels (*Revenge of the Creature*, 1955; *The Creature Walks Among Us*, 1956) bring the now-famous Creature into the everyday world (destruction is usually negated when a theme proves popular enough for a sequel). In the final of the Creature films, the monster is operated upon so as to be able to exist longer in air, tamed, and even dressed as a man. However, he eventually reverts, proving, perhaps, the implacability of deviation as a threat to society and the impracticality of coexistence.

In this group of films, the normal environment plays a far greater role in the mood, behavior, and motivation than it does in more atmospheric films. It is also the closest to other genres, such as science-fiction. The hero of the bipartite movie is far more competent, and deals with threats by more modern means, not by methodologically surrendering to the rules as set by his monster-antagonist, as is the case in most atmospheric films.

Other examples of bipartite films are *Curse of the Cat People* (1944), *Vampire's Ghost* (set in a jungle milieu, 1945), *The Thing* (1951), *Attack of the Crab Monsters* (1957), and *The Mysterians* (1959).

Social Monster Movies

The problems of our so-called other-directed, conformist society, emphasized in the works of Reisman and others, are immediately and obviously connected to social monster films, which are permeated by stultifying pressures for conformity. (This is due—at least in part—to the fact that the new teenage market equates realism with the definition and justification of its values.)

Giant Gila Monster (1959) is a very typical recent social monster movie (as are almost all of those regarding giant snails, turtles, crabs, grasshoppers, ants, scorpions, bees, mantises, octopi, amoebas, shrews, assorted spiders aplenty, and people of various sorts), with more social overtones than most. These overtones include the juvenile delinquent hero obtaining a lucrative contract as a result of singing "The Gila Monster Rock." The monster-plot itself is only part of the entire socialization of the hero, as he learns that deviants are automatically to be destroyed when found, and that this action produces happiness to all conformists.

In *Teenage Zombies* (1960) the teenagers are monsters only because and so long as they are forced out of their usual social role; through their eventual and inevitable return to conformity and the celebration of Society Triumphant, they become heroes. The zombiemakers (who perform their evils by use of a complex electronic machine) are vaguely identified as representing a foreign power. By making the heroes and heroines into zombies they destroy their individual liberties (to conform), and thus represent the drive toward deviance and a threat to the American Way. They are treated as monsters, and destroyed. This type of theme is clearly amenable to treatment by the zombie film, of which many have been made throughout all three horror film periods.

In *Godzilla, King of the Monsters* (1956) and *Gigantis, the Fire Monster* (1959), a sequel, the motivation of the monster is that of society itself toward deviance and deviants—the drive to simply destroy anything different from itself. These strange, destructive creatures are finally pacified only when society draws upon its ultimate secret hardware.

Gorgo (1961) has a very unusual ending, in that the monster actually wins the day against all opposition. Nonetheless, the monster mother and her baby (who has been kidnapped by society) are alone and, if not defenseless, completely within society's environment. Their own home is the depths of the sea, to which they return, after the baby's becoming lost and the mother's foray into society to free it. Thus, whether the monster is brought into or comes into conflict with mankind has little effect on the treatment and mood of the film as a whole. This film is a sort of moral lesson, a "cry in the wilderness" against our overweening selfishness (as a group) which attempts to subjugate all deviant values, or even accepted values (such as Mother Love) if held by deviants, to the goals of the Mass.

Other social monster movies include *The Magnetic Monster* (1953), *Abbott and Costello Meet the Mummy* (1955), *Kronos* (1957), *Blood of Dracula* (1957), *Teenage Cave Man* (1958), *Night of the Blood Beast* (1958), *Frankenstein—1970* (1958), and *Curse of the Werewolf* (1961).

There is no clear-cut trichotomy in this categorization of monster movies, but rather a continuum. Along this, realism is correlated with movies toward the social end of the scale, unrealism with those toward the atmospheric. Morality is equated with the social end, immorality (or amorality in a more objective sense) with the atmospheric. The presentation of double standards of behavior is more typical of the bipartite monster movie.

Atmospheric monster movies appeal more directly to those with antisocial feelings or values (in the meaning of deviant mores, not necessarily of hostile intent); bipartite ones to those who are more objective, or in an asocial mood; social ones to those who need their acceptance of and faith in society's mores strengthened and justified in their own minds.

The Puritan Despair
by MICHEL PEREZ

I Walked with a Zombie is an admirably apt title for a film that
proves romantic to the point of frenzy. As a work, too, of unusual
beauty, this film is doubly hard to account for, given the seemingly
wondrous spontaneity of its means and effects. In its means and effects the film shows, furthermore, the confluence of two equally
strong currents in the commercial Hollywood cinema: one, the
regular series of horror movies produced from its early days on by
Universal Films; the other, a line of films which began appearing
about 1940—ten years after Universal's first cycle of horror sound
films—a line which owes rather more to Freud than to Mary Shelley
or Bram Stoker. The film's sources are to be found, then, in both the
horror fantasy and the psychological thriller: effects common to both
converge in its chiaroscuro. Not that the film seeks to throw a clinical
light on the dark mysteries it evokes, mysteries rooted and entwined
in the cult of Voodoo and in the sexual manners, even more tene-
brous and labyrinthine than the domain of Voodoo, of the Victorian woman. The burden of sexual frustration which pervades
the atmosphere of *I Walked with a Zombie,* as of so many American
films, is inherent in the plot; it is assumed as given. The film develops as a tapestry of frustration: the forlorn sexuality which is its
determining motif is comparable in its enmeshing weave to the web
spun by a spider or to the design—a design it would be wrong to
describe unqualifiedly as hideous—formed by the wavering curved
tentacles of an octopus. In the grip of this design, as in the grip of
the voracious petals of some carnivorous and poisonous flower, slowly
expanding to encompass it, an entire world is consumed.

From Positif, *no. 92 (February 1968): 61–63. Copyright © 1968 by
Editions le Terrain Vague. English translation by T. J. Ross copyright
© 1972 by T. J. Ross. Used by permission of the publisher.*

We behold the heroine of the film so consumed herself by catatonic seizures as to verge on being a living corpse: a sleepwalker in a lace winding sheet, she wanders along a moonlit beach to the sound of Voodoo drums, her mind as bereft of dreams as of reason, lacking both in lucidity and in visionary passion; yet it is she, bloodless, haggard, sapped by fever, who becomes for us the supreme object—and most beautiful imaginable—of our erotic desires. The sort of dizzying necrophilia here instanced overwhelms not only the characters of the film but also us in the audience as we gradually succumb to the decadent force of the film's images.

This film, directed by Jacques Tourneur, appeared several years after Alfred Hitchcock's *Rebecca*. And though Tourneur himself may not have been directly influenced by the sweeping success of *Rebecca,* it is clear that the producers of *I Walked with a Zombie* were aiming indeed at the freshly exploitable market for films dealing in ghostly presences, or the mad, or other such demonic types who are regularly delivered up as fodder to the more ravaging expectations of the puritan imagination. Predictably, then, the scenario of the film turns out to be fashioned in accord with the basic rules of true-romance stories. And so we find—set off against our spectral figure—a full-bodied, appallingly healthy type with whom stout-hearted readers (or spectators) of either sex may at once identify; for though the hardy spectator doesn't see himself as one likely to become enamored of a phantom being, he does relish seeing himself in the role of nurse or guardian to such a type. It is one of the curious corollaries of the stark ambiguities of puritanism. It is to be expected therefore that the dauntless nurse summoned to watch over the invalid should become so involved with her patient through her own all-consuming empathy as to fall violently in love with her patient's husband. Yet she dares not act on her obsession, nor even articulate it to herself, until the actual death of the living-dead creature (the extremity of whose own state is indeed at a point beyond recall to life). Throughout, the nurse remains devoted to the phantom in her care with a grimly self-abnegating passion.

The conflicts thereby engendered—the Corneille-like torments, the remorse, the melodramatic seesawing back and forth from the compulsions of the flesh to the jabs of conscience, the consequent doubts and anguish—are of a kind to encourage our apprehending the action altogether in novelettish terms.

The film in fact escapes and transcends the bathos of true romance precisely through its intensive morbidity and its steady focus

on the rituals of Voodoo. Numerous scenes, to be sure, would border
on soap opera, were it not for the atmosphere they generate, an atmosphere whose dominant visual and sound elements—the unyield-
ing and maleficent glare of the moonlight in counterpoint with the
overriding background beat of Voodoo drums—combine rather
to reflect a general psychosexual imbalance comparable in its ver-
tigo to the flounderings of, and the sensations experienced by, a
drowning man. It is as if one were trying to lift oneself out of a
whirlpool by one's cries alone, in a mad hope of hurling oneself back
to solid land, before being again engulfed in this recurring nightmare as by a menacing wave at the crest. Hidden in the message of
the nightmare is that Dream against which the Whites pose every
sort of defense but which the Blacks daily abide by in the simplicity
of their ceremonial codes. Accepting the supernatural, they live in
the innocence of a magic world whose dangers are known and liable
to control by the most rigorously observed means. We may identify
the Dream as a dream of self at ease with its sexuality, unblocked
by the taboos and inhibitions of civilization. For the Whites the
surrounding world is hostile, its dangers the same as for the Blacks,
but without the possibilities of their exorcism, since it is forbidden
to the Whites to seek antidotes to their anguish in magic sources.
There is neither remedy nor solace for the puritan despair.

We find no traces of colonialist sentiment nor of racism in *I
Walked with a Zombie*; nor any condescension in its depiction of
surviving tribal customs, nor in the fact that the enactments of the
customs and ceremonies are presented as disturbing, vaguely (or
deliberately) monstrous, recalling the sort of "savage" scenes often
sketched for adventure books of the Victorian period. These dis-
orienting and exotic aspects of the scene serve to confront and contain the entourage of hounded Whites, as they turn their eyes to the
dark flames of the Voodoo.

Evil, magic, witchcraft—these are not at the heart of the film's
interests and concerns. In no sense are the Whites the victims of
Voodoo priests; nor can the latter in any way effect their cure. What
is central is the dramatic confrontation which is sparked by the conjunction of two equally romantic literary traditions. A confrontation
transfigured by cinematic means into a poem whose beauty is inseparable from its despair.

"Gobble, Gobble... One of Us!"
by JOHN THOMAS

First released in this country in 1932, Tod Browning's *Freaks* quickly vanished into the maw of the 42nd St. movie houses, there to be spat out as indigestible by puzzled audiences who found other Browning films like *Dracula* and *Mark of the Vampire* more comprehensibly horrifying. The film then went to Europe, where it slowly gained a reputation that gradually filtered back to the United States, raising some interest but few revivals. Finally, at the 1962 Cannes Festival Repertory, *Freaks* was selected to represent the horror film category, and later in the year played for the first time in Great Britain. Now, after more than 30 years, it has come back to the country of its birth.

Since most revivals are disappointing, let it be said from the outset that *Freaks* will disappoint no one but the mindless children who consume most horror films. *Freaks* is, in its own way, a minor masterpiece. Certainly it is macabre, and the final sequence in which the freaks stalk and mutilate their victims is enough to scare the hell out of anybody. But the point is that *Freaks* is not really a horror film at all, though it contains some horrifying sequences. The conventional horror film is one of our responses to the nonhuman element in the world, the incomprehensible objective world that threatens to render life meaningless. The movie monster is the embodiment of the nonhuman, the irrational, the inexplicable. It is through his destruction by fire, sunlight, or crucifix that we are purged of our own fear of the nonhuman. We must therefore identify with the victims of the movie monster, and find our release in the monster's ultimate death. In *Freaks* we are asked to

Appeared originally as "Freaks," in Film Quarterly, *17, no. 3 (Spring 1964): 59–61. Copyright © 1964 by the Regents of the University of California. Reprinted by permission of the Regents and the author.*

identify with the ostensibly nonhuman, to turn against what we normally think of as our "own kind" and to discover in the humanity of the freaks a moral center for the universe.

The routine plot is merely a structure upon which Browning can work to achieve this remarkable reversal. Hans, a circus midget, is engaged to Frieda, another midget, but is attracted to Cleopatra, an Amazon high-wire performer. Cleopatra is enjoying her own affair with Hercules, the circus strong man, but encourages Hans because of the secret pleasure she finds in ridiculing him. When she discovers that Hans has inherited a large fortune, she plans with Hercules to marry the midget and then poison him. The plot is discovered, and the other freaks hunt down the villains and mutilate them, transforming Cleopatra herself into a freak.

Apart from the normal players, most of the roles are taken by real circus freaks assembled by Browning from all over the world—dwarfs, midgets, pinheads, bearded ladies, human worms, Siamese twins.

The crucial scenes in the movie are those which show the daily routine of the freaks, the individual adjustment of the freaks to their handicaps being almost clinically observed. We watch the armless woman drink beer from a glass grasped by a prehensile foot; while the human worm, both armless and legless, lights his own cigarettes with his teeth. Having selected a new dress, the pinhead Slitzy flirts charmingly with the clown—Wallace Ford, one of the few normal characters who treats the freaks as equals, and acts as a link between the two worlds. Slitzy's normal womanly reactions are matched by those of Frieda, whose romance with Hans is so managed as to appear more mature, more dignified, despite squeaky voices and stiff gestures, than the comparable affair of Cleopatra and Hercules. It is through these and similar scenes that Browning effects the inversion of values that lies at the heart of the film.

The freaks, as the movie is at pains to point out, live in a world of their own, created by themselves, but open to all of their own kind and to any normal person good enough to accept them. They are very much in this world, determined to make the best of it. It is only the nonaccepting attitude of some of the normals which precipitates the crisis that finally turns those normals themselves into freaks.

What, then, are we to make of this as a "horror" film? Can the freaks be seen both as objects of sympathy and as nightmarish incarnations of the nonhuman? Browning does evoke both responses, creating a tension within the viewer which could ruin the movie but which in fact enriches it. The use of the freaks for the creation of macabre effects is skillful enough, but always, until the last scene, mixed with a warm appreciation of their humanity.

For instance, we are first introduced to them during an outing in the country, when the camera, peering through the trees, comes upon a grotesque round dance of hopping, squirming, crawling things. Then, as the camera draws closer, the monsters resolve suddenly into people—"just children," as the normal woman with them explains—transformed from agents of terror to objects of compassion within moments.

Then there is the justifiably famous wedding feast, with Cleopatra and Hercules the only normals present, a ritual celebration of freak culture. Leading a macabre chant, "We accept her, we accept her, gobble gobble, one of us, one of us," a dwarf dances across the banquet table bearing a huge communal wine bowl, offering it at last to Cleopatra to drink from as her token of induction into the world of the freaks. There can be no surprise at Cleopatra's revulsion at this point, but any sympathy one might have for her collapses as she later humiliates Hans in front of his friends by riding him about on her shoulders. Once again the openness of the freaks is contrasted with the intolerance and false security of the "normals."

Certainly the final sequence in which the freaks hunt down and mutilate Cleopatra and Hercules is as ghoulish as anyone could wish. Amidst a jumble of wrecked circus trailers, lightning splitting sky and sound track, the ground a muddy ooze, the darkness swarms with crawling, hopping shapes, lit grotesquely by momentary flashes, all humanity seemingly erased.

This is our last image of the freaks, and perhaps it may be counted an artistic mistake. If the picture is really an attempt to evoke sympathy, can it end with the freaks transformed into monsters?

It can, and does, because the ground has been so carefully prepared that the audience must, at the end of the film, react against its own revulsion. We are horrified, but we are simultaneously ashamed of our horror; for we remember that these are not monsters at all but people like us, and we know that we have again been betrayed by our own primal fears. Had the picture ended on a more idyllic note, we might have been self-satisfied, stuffed with our own tolerant virtue. Instead, we are plunged back into the abyss of our own sick selves, to recall once again that the most fearful inhumanity we can know is our own. With this final scene, then, the double image is complete. Each of them is one of us; each of us, one of them.

PSYCHOLOGICAL THRILLER

Val Lewton and the School
of Shudders
by MANNY FARBER

The death of Val (Vladimir) Lewton, Hollywood's top producer of B movies, occurred during the final voting on 1951's outstanding film contributors. The proximity of these two events underlines the significant fact that Lewton's horror productions (*Death Ship, The Body Snatcher, Isle of the Dead*), which always conveyed a very visual, unorthodox artistry, were never recognized as "Oscar" worthy. On the other hand, in acclaiming people like Ferrer, Mankiewicz, and Holliday, the industry has indicated its esteem for bombshells who disorganize the proceedings on the screen with their flamboyant eccentricities and relegate the camera to the role of passive bit player.

Lewton always seemed a weirdly misplaced figure in Hollywood. He specialized in gentle, scholarly, well-wrought productions that were as modest in their effects as his estimate of himself. Said he: "Years ago I wrote novels for a living, and when RKO was looking for producers, someone told them I had written horrible novels. They misunderstood the word horrible for horror and I got the job." Having taken on the production of low-cost thrillers (budgeted under $500,000) about pretty girls who turn into man-eating cats or believe in zombies, Lewton started proving his odd idea, for a celluloid entertainer, that "a picture can never be too good for the public." This notion did not spring from a desire to turn out original, noncommercial films, for Lewton never possessed that

Appeared originally as "Val Lewton, 1951," in Negative Space *by Manny Farber (New York: Praeger Publications, Inc., 1971), pp. 47–50. Copyright © 1971 by Manny Farber. Reprinted by permission of Praeger Publications, Inc. and Studio Vista Publishers.*

kind of brilliance or ambition; it came instead from a pretty reasonable understanding of his own limitations. Unlike the majority
of Hollywood craftsmen, he was so bad at supplying the kind of
"punch" familiar to American films that the little mayhem he did
manage was crude, poorly motivated, and as incredible as the Music
Hall make-up on his Indians in *Apache Drums*—the last and least
of his works. He also seemed to have a psychological fear of creating
expensive effects, so that his stock in trade became the imparting of
much of the story through such low-cost suggestions as frightening
shadows. His talents were those of a mild bibliophile whose idea of
"good" cinema had too much to do with using quotes from
Shakespeare or Donne, bridging scenes with a rare folk song, cap-
turing climate with a description of a West Indian dish, and, in the
pensive sequences, making sure a bit player wore a period mouth
instead of a modern lipsticky one. Lewton's efforts not infrequently
suggested a minor approximation of *Jane Eyre*.

The critics who called Lewton the "Sultan of Shudders" and
"Chill-master" missed the deliberate quality of his insipidly normal
characters, who reminded one of the actors used in smalltown movie
ads for the local grocery or shoe store. Lewton and his scriptwriters
collaborated on sincere, adult pulp stories, which gave sound bits
of knowledge on subjects like zoanthropia or early English asylums
while steering almost clear of formula horror.

The Curse of the Cat People, for instance, was simply for the
overconscientious parent of a problem child. The film concerns a
child (Ann Carter) who worries or antagonizes the people around
her with her daydreaming; the more they caution and reprimand,
the more she withdraws to the people of her fantasies for "friends."
When she finds an old photograph of her father's deceased, psychopathic first wife (Simone Simon, the cat woman of an earlier film),
she sees her as one of her imagined playmates; the father fears his
daughter has become mentally ill and is under a curse. His insistence that she stop daydreaming brings about the climax, and the
film's conclusion is that he should have more trust and faith in his
daughter and her visions. Innocuous plots such as these were fashioned with peculiar ingredients that gave them an air of genteel
sensitivity and enchantment; there was the dry documenting of a
bookworm, an almost delicate distrust of excitement, economical
camera and sound effects, as well as fairy-tale titles and machinations. The chilling factor came from the perverse process of in-
jecting tepid thrills with an eyedropper into a respectable story, a

technique Lewton and his favorite scriptwriter, Donald Henderson Clarke, picked up during long careers writing sex shockers for drug-store book racks. While skittering daintily away from concrete evidences of cat woman or brutality, they would concentrate with the fascination of a voyeur on unimportant bric-a-brac, reflections, domestic animals, so that the camera would take on the faintly un-healthy eye of a fetishist. The morbidity came from the obsessive preoccupation with which writers and cameramen brought out the voluptuous reality of things, such as a dangerously swinging ship's hook, which was inconspicuously knocking men overboard like tenpins.

Lewton's most accomplished maneuver was making the audience think much more about his material than it warranted. Some of his devices were the usual ones of hiding information, having his people murdered offstage, or cutting into a murderous moment in a gloomy barn with a shot of a horse whinnying. He, however, hid much more of his story than any other filmmaker, and forced his crew to create drama almost abstractly with symbolic sounds, tex-tures, and the like, which made the audience hyperconscious of sensitive craftsmanship. He imperiled his characters in situations that didn't call for outsized melodrama and permitted the use of a journalistic camera—for example, a sailor trying to make himself heard over the din of a heavy chain that is burying him inside a ship's locker. He would use a spray-shot technique that usually con-sisted of oozing suggestive shadows across a wall, or watching the heroine's terror on a lonely walk, and then add a homey wind-up of the cat woman trying to clean her conscience in a bathtub decorated with cat paws. This shorthand method allowed Lewton to ditch the laughable aspects of improbable events and give the remaining bits of material the strange authenticity of a daguerrotype.

The Leopard Man is a cleaner and much less sentimental Lewton, sticking much more to the suspense element and misdirection, using some of his favorite images, people moving in a penitential, sleep-walking manner, episodes threaded together with a dramatic sound. This fairly early peak example of his talent is a nerve-twitching whodunit giving the creepy impression that human beings and "things" are interchangeable and almost synonymous and that both are pawns of a bizarre and terrible destiny. A lot of surrealists like Cocteau have tried for the same supernatural effects, but, while their scenes still seem like portraits in motion, Val Lewton's film shows a way to tell a story about people that isn't dominated by the activity, weight, size, and pace of the human figure. In one segment of the film, a small frightened señorita walks beyond the edge of the border town and then back again, while her feelings and imagination keep shifting with the camera into sagebrush, the darkness of an arroyo, crackling pebbles underfoot, and so on, until you see her thick dark blood oozing under the front door of her house. All the psychological effects—fear and so on—were transformed by Tourneur into nonhuman components of the picture as the girl waited for some noncorporeal manifestation of nature, culture, or history to gobble her up. But, more important in terms of movie invention, Lewton's use of multiple focus (characters are dropped or picked up as if by chance, while the movie goes off on odd tacks trying to locate a sound or a suspicion) and his lighter-than-air sense of pace created a terrifically plastic camera style. It put the camera eye on a curiously delicate wave length that responds to scenery as quickly as the mind, and gets inside of people instead of reacting only to surface qualities. This film still seems to be one of Hollywood's original gems—nothing impure in terms of cinema, nothing imitative about its style, and little that misses fire through a lack of craft.

Unfortunately, his directors (he discovered Robson and Wise in the cutting department) became so delirious about scenic camera work that they used little imagination on the acting. But the sterile performances were partly due to Lewton's unexciting idea that characters should always be sweet, "like the people who go to the movies"—a notion that slightly improved such veteran creeps as Karloff, but stopped the more pedantic actors (Kent Smith, Daniell) dead in their tracks. Lewton's distinction always came from his sense of the soundly constructed novel; his $200,000 jobs are so skillfully engineered in pace, action, atmosphere that they have lost little of the haunting effect they had when released years ago.

The Terror of the Surreal

by CARL BELZ

We shall be plunged normally into the marvelous

NOËL ARNAUD

A resurgent interest in the artistic movements which dominated the first half of the twentieth century, particularly Dada and Surrealism, has taught us that both implied a "way of seeing" as well as directing our attention toward specific areas of subject matter. While both possessed a special style, one whose aims very often involved elements of shock and surprise, neither limited itself to one medium alone. Neither did they create any bounds on the range of objects from which could be drawn a creative inspiration. While the discarded paraphernalia of everyday life offered Dadaists an harmonious counterpart for a nihilistic point of view, Surrealism often began with a less dramatic vocabulary, although by recombining words and forms, transformed it into a vehicle for fantasy.

In both movements photographers and filmmakers occupied a small but important area, adding notable contributions to the respective ranges of vision. The photogram technique, employed by Man Ray and Lazlo Maholy-Nagy, produced, as early as 1921, the first abstract photographs. This was the same year that Hans Richter offered, with *Rhythmus 21*, an archetype for non-objective film. Throughout the twenties a mixture of the Dada and Surrealist points of view could be found in such classics as Fernand Léger's *Ballet Mechanique*, Man Ray's *Emak Bakia*, or René Clair and Francis Picabia's *Entr'acte*. It was at the end of the decade, however, that three films emerged which demonstrated Surrealism's

Appeared originally as "The Birds," in Film Culture, *no. 31 (Winter 1963–64): 51–53. Copyright © 1964 by* Film Culture. *Reprinted by permission of* Film Culture.

ability to create dreams and visions in the film medium: the two collaborative efforts of Luis Buñuel and Salvador Dali, *Chien Andalou* and *L'Age d'Or,* and Jean Cocteau's *Le Sang d'un Poète.*

The films mentioned above have generally been characterized as "experimental," a term which, until recently, has provided the most convenient distinction between serious cinema artists and their more public-oriented Hollywood brethren. That the term is more convenient than meaningful has been pointed out by various critics: the work of individuals like Resnais or Antonioni provides convincing evidence that commercial films can also offer the battleground for new ideas. They likewise demonstrate that, without being formally Surrealistic, the legacy of this style continues to bear artistic fruit. The deserted town through which Sandro and Claudia pass in *L'Avventura,* for example, possesses a starkness and mystery akin to the dreamy city-scapes of the early de Chirico. Resnais' Marienbad world is likewise enshrouded with an other-worldly mystery; the entire film is, on one level of experience, like an escapade into the surreality of dreams or remembrances where the relationship between parts is fragmentary and evasive.

Emotional shock and psychological chaos are two additional aspects of Surrealism's many-faceted expression. The Dali-Buñuel films present this side of the movement with graphic and undeniable clarity. An unabashed eroticism is likewise a standard element in the Surrealist vocabulary. In Alfred Hitchcock's *The Birds,* as in the earlier *Psycho,* one views his personal brand of eroticism as well as his interpretation of expressive human experience. "Thriller" is the category into which much of Hitchcock's work is all too quickly shuffled. It is only recently in this country that critics and audiences have begun to seek out the more engaging undercurrents of meaning and implication in Hitchcock's films. The trend has been given an additional impetus through the Museum of Modern Art's retrospective showing of his productions.

The Birds offers a case in point, an experience which exists on various artistic and conceptual levels. The viewer who anticipates a "shocker" or a "thriller" comes off with a very conventional example of this genre; many critics disparaged the film for this very reason. One anticipates rather early in the film the attacks which are about to take place; they happen, and only occasionally in some unexpected manner: for example, the cascade of birds through the fireplace and into the living room. It is the contention of the present discussion, however, that such moments are of secondary importance, and that the total work must be viewed as a fantasy which uses reality only as a sort of convenient launching pad, going beyond it into a sur-real sphere of human existence. The method of the film, in fact, shares much with surrealistic expression in general.

Typically surrealist is the way in which a plot of the most ordinary dimension provides the foundation for a superstructure of artistic experience. Nothing could be more conventional than the eternal "boy (with mother) meets girl" situation. The secondary characters are equally unimaginative: a younger sister who is immediately attracted to the girl, and a school teacher, the former but still interested and would-be partner for the virile hero. Comparable examples of superficially ordinary situations may be cited from various artists whose work shows surrealist inclinations. In film, Jean Vigo, in *Zero de Conduit,* and Jean Cocteau, in *Le Sang d'un Poète,* employ typical situations with children—a dormitory adventure or a school yard snowball fight—and, in each case, extract from them a sense of the marvelous. René Magritte's painting does likewise, utilizing a nude torso, an easel painting, or still life objects, which, through a recombination of the parts, become fantastic, enigmatic, and symbolic landscapes.

A disturbing "aura" also surrounds Hitchcock's characters. They are typical to the point of being unreal. In a sense they are impossible, like meeting the average man-composites of their respective sexes and generations, cross sections which one idealizes from statistics, but which do not exist in the pure state presented by the film. The sequence in the cafe has the same quality: drunk, bar tender, salesman, frightened mother with two children, sea captain, and ornithologist. Each is a stereotype; to find them, let alone finding them all together, strains the viewer's credulity. With such a scene we cross the delicate line separating the real from the sur-real; this is dramatic fantasy. With a rising sense of expectation one wonders if each character will say and do that which would be expected from knowing the definition of him; when he does, it is like having the perennial bad dream come true, like the uneasiness one experiences when he senses that all this has happened before, or in some evasive dream.

The unreal quality of the characters seems heightened by the use of color in this film. Whereas black and white might have softened the appearances, color seems to heighten each visage: the freckles of the little girl, the gaudy, pasty make-up of the women, the bronze tan of the hero. Once again the "natural" is intensified to a point where it borders on the super-natural.

An important aspect of surrealism is the tension which is created between the appearance of things and their role in the total work. Such a tension is most obvious in the double image or visual pun popular among such painters as Dali or Magritte. More subtle, however, are the works of de Chirico. In these city views each element is clearly expressed, each is immediately recognizable. We may see, for instance, a deserted street, an arcade, a lonely tower, statue, or clock. But atop the tower a banner ripples in the wind, and at the end of the street a train passes in the night. The combination of elements is alarming and creates an atmosphere of mystery and dreamy enchantment. In the midst of utter stillness, the wind blows; in an otherwise deserted city one figure remains; a locomotive proceeds to some unknown destination. The resulting experience is one of paradox and ambiguity; questions are stated, but nothing is resolved.

Hitchcock's film is likewise wrought with tensions and ambiguities. Despite the simplicity of the characters, they form, as artistic units, no coherent whole. The entire subplot dealing with the school teacher seems out of context with the general flow of the narrative, and adds nothing to it. The incident involving the store keeper also appears overelaborated. The mother, lying in bed after the shock of discovering the body of the slaughtered farmer, suddenly begins talking about her former husband. Again, this has little bearing on, or relationship to, the central theme of the film. As the viewer tries to reconcile these events, to perceive the relationship between the disparate parts, tensions arise from the lack of unity. One wonders about the disjunction of these various sections, the number of self-contained but non-functional units. As in the example of de Chirico, or in any number of Surrealist works where individually understandable elements form a whole which remains a series of tenuously related fragments, The Birds relies on an unconventional logic, that which Baudelaire termed "the logic of the absurd."

Paradox, in fact, is fundamental to the surrealist point of view. Its role in surrealist thought has been clearly stated by André Breton in his second manifesto: "There is a certain point for the mind from which life and death, the real and the imaginary, the past and the future, the communicable and the incommunicable, the high and the low cease being perceived as contradictions." For the surrealists, then, opposed elements become harmonized, and the marvelous takes place before our eyes.

That *The Birds* represents a flight into the realm of fantasy and not simply a suspense or science fiction thriller may be indicated by investigating another feature of surrealist thought: its complete detachment from rhetorical function. A characteristic aspect of the science fiction idiom is the "point" which is all too often hammered home at the viewer: the danger in misunderstanding the space visitors, or the mad genius scientist; or the hazards inherent in the experiment which has not been fully plotted. With surrealism, however, "the image," as Wallace Fowlie points out, "must not be useful; it must be innocent. Surrealist art must be stripped of rhetoric: it must never seek to prove anything."

The Birds, then, represents an extraordinary film experience. On one level it conforms to a typical breed of the American cinema. On a deeper level, however, it exhibits qualities of tension and ambiguity, contradictions which suggest that the reality portrayed is of a special variety. The particular nature of these contradictions, the conflict between the reality of the parts and the unreality of the whole, produces an encounter with the fantastic, a picture of the world beyond the real, in short, of the sur-real.

A New Ending to ROSEMARY'S BABY
by RAY BRADBURY

I went back to see *Rosemary's Baby* the other night. I had to go back. I mean, everyone is. Just as everyone is going back to *2001: A Space Odyssey*. Not to go back, not to look again, not to figure it out is commensurate with saying, a few years ago, you hadn't read Salinger, or this year, Tolkien.

Sitting there in the dark watching, I felt the same sense of dissatisfaction. The truth is I simply do not believe or accept the ending of *Rosemary's Baby*.

In case you have forgotten, or never knew, here's how the last reel of the film stacks up.

Rosemary, having been raped by her husband, poisoned by next-door neighbors who raise exotic milk drinks in the kitchen, double-crossed by one doctor and bilked by another, gives birth to a child which vanishes, reported dead.

Hearing a baby cry beyond her bedroom wall, she breaks into the next apartment where she finds husband, neighbors, doctor, and the child: Satan Reborn amidst festivities and happy cries of "God is dead!"

Though Rosemary carries with her a fine sharp carving knife, she does nothing with it. When asked to shush and rock the blasphemous child, she does so. Fade out. THE END.

Nonsense. Also: balderdash.

On a purely paranoid level, the woman would have to kill someone: her husband, a neighbor who poisoned her, a doctor who lied to her, or the baby itself.

If we take the film on a non-psychological level, as pure fantasy,

From Films and Filming *August 1969, p. 10. Copyright © 1969 by Ray Bradbury. Reprinted by permission of the Harold Matson Company, Inc.*

it still doesn't work. In severe shock, sore put upon by a witch's gaggle of villains, you don't sit down amidst panic to rock nightmare.

What then should the ending of *Rosemary's Baby* be?

I dare to offer the following:

CLOSE-UP: Rosemary, knife in hand, frozen in the midst of the satanic jubilee.

She approaches the cradle where the strange and terrible child stirs.

Everyone gasps. What will she do?

Kill the child? Attack her husband or one of them?

No.

She drops the knife, seizes the babe in her arms and whirls. Is she going to throw the child out the window?

No, she runs out the door, into the elevator, and down into the street. The Satanists pursue, fearful and shouting.

A light drizzling rain is falling at dusk in New York. No thunder, no lightning; no Gothic super-effects, just a soft drizzle through which Rosemary runs, shielding her babe from the rain, and behind, the devil-pack in full cry.

She turns, runs, turns again, down alleys, up streets until at last she reaches a church or (why not?) a cathedral.

In she runs!

The Satanists gather at every door, on all sides. Afraid to enter, they hover on the sill, soaked by rain, faces dripping, peering in at:

Rosemary, who runs up the main aisle of the cathedral, reaches the great altar, and stops, unveiling the child.

What will she do now?

The worshippers of evil watch from every door. The rain whispers on the cold stones.

Rosemary steps up upon the altar platform and holds the baby out and up in the air and at last, eyes shut, gathers courage to speak. And this is what she says:

"O Lord, O God, O Lord God. Take back your Son!"

Silence. Rain.

Pull the camera back slowly, and up into the high reaches of the cathedral where we can see Rosemary and her baby on the altar, praying, waiting, and, in every door, cold and rain-drenched, the demon people.

Fade to black. The End.

And *that*, my friends, is the way *Rosemary's Baby* should have ended.

Which then would have sent audiences out into the night to think what kind of idea had just run over them.

Which then would have sent everyone home to crack the Old Testament or probe through *Paradise Lost* after Milton's Dark Angel.

You think not? I think so. How resist such a delicious concept? How could one go to sleep that night without tracking down the Devil's genealogy?

For, after all, wasn't there a time, billions of æons ago, when Lucifer stood by the Throne of God? Was he not an accepted Angel? Was he not one of the Sons? And, at one time, did he not dare to use his intelligence and power, testing God? And in so doing, was he not cast out of Heaven and hurled to the fiery pit to sweat out the millennia? All this he was, all this he did, all this he suffered.

And, finally, then, does not God forgive? And dark-hooved child brought by blameless and sore-tried mother onto a cathedral altar on rainy night; could God refuse such needful prayers? Would not the Lord take back his ancient enemy and make of him once more a Son upon the right hand of the Throne?

There is my script, my new and inevitable FINIS. Film it in your mind. Screen it on your eyelids tonight.

Then turn and walk out of the cinema, the cathedral, with me.

Leaving Rosemary there, with her sad child, waiting for answers which *must* come.

Polanski,
REPULSION,
and the New Mythology
by T. J. ROSS

Two sisters share a flat in London, where they have come from across the channel to live. Yvonne Furneaux plays the brunette and bumptious older sister. The other, played by Catherine Deneuve, is ingrained to the point of madness. Blonde and of a striking yet immobile beauty, she works in a beauty salon as a manicurist, and it is her story with which *Repulsion* deals.

Her psychosis, manifest in the fury of her recoil from men, puts her off the normal rhythms and schemes of her scene, puts her at an angle to the everyday scene which is close to that of a poet's—a mad poet's, yet a poet's nonetheless: no T. S. Eliot or J. D. Salinger could be more fiercely conscious of, nor feel more vulnerable to, the grosser—"fleshpot"—aspects of the life of the city. In our heroine's case, she is in recoil from the whole world outside her room, which she sees in anthropomorphic terms as the Villain. It is the villainy of the world to which she feels prey to a degree which makes her delirious. And the world lurking outside her room is first symbolized for her in the shaving equipment left on the washstand by her sister's lover. Then it threatens in the form of gigantic hands which poke through the walls to clutch at her; or else, it is as a sundering of the walls in lightning-like cracks. Finally, it is in the images of men which loom with an equal suddenness in her mirror. And when these last images in fact become real, she will be compelled to act with more than a shudder and blink of the eyes.

From Film Heritage *4, no. 2 (Winter 1968–69): 1–10. Copyright ©
1969 by F. A. Macklin. Reprinted by permission of* Film Heritage *and
the author.*

Locked into herself she is indeed at the mercy of the world, her imbalance signalled in the severity of her response to the razor and shaving mug. (Besides her sister, the one person with whom she is ever shown at ease is a plain co-worker at the salon, unselfconscious and in distress over her own troubles with a boyfriend, who joins with the heroine in a momentary let-up of gossip and giggles.)

Where the poet strikes back through the aggression and assertion of his art, our psychotic beauty is mute. Her mode of expression can only be one of speechless violence. She is like a Dracula, each of whose emergences from the casket of self heralds an act of horror. In its bleak humor the plot works to suggest, however, that what she is driven mad by—and what finally drives her to murder—is in line with what exacerbates and drives a poet to creation.

Through the first part of the film our heroine is courted by a youth seemingly well suited to the role of the Prince Charming who rouses the beauty from her trance. When not in pursuit of the girl, this Nice Guy type is seen in his pub with his friends, one of whom, a Hail-Fellow-Well-Met, continually harps on the theme that there is more than one fish in the ocean. Completing this company is a goggled-eyed, long-jawed character who slobbers at Hail-Fellow's stories and joins him in twitting Nice Guy for his unwonted mooniness.

This kidding of Nice Guy occurs at a point in the film when we in the audience have been won over to his cause, cheering for him to win over the girl. And since we have been led to understand her external responses in relation to her inner distress, the girl too will have won much of our sympathetic interest: she is in fact the only character who is given the dimensions—however curious—of an inner life.

Where Nice Guy ordinarily would have gone along with the gags, he on this occasion gets violent, grabbing Goggle-Eyes by the throat. Hail-Fellow intervenes and seeks to make amends by assuring his friend that he "loves" him still and playfully giving him a loud kiss full on the lips: which again is not accepted in the jovial spirit intended. Nice Guy starts back in a shock of repulsion. Through his enchantment with the girl, he has become disoriented in his own usual way of vision and response, has become less tolerant of the casual high jinks and brutishness of the mundane world. He has become intense.

For in a previous scene, when he had leaned over the wheel of his sports car to kiss the girl, she had recoiled with the same dismay and look of shocked revelation as he at the bar from Hail-Fellow. The balance of the two scenes is clear; their point, a bit more difficult. Easy enough for us to assume here a point of contrast rather than one of tenuous comparison; we want to see the heroine accept the kiss which will bring her to life in the world. But Nice Guy himself is no St. George or R. D. Laing, no match for the monsters in her mind. He is out of his league; and he carries too the stigma of the pub, of the public world into which he would draw her. His recoil in the pub is sprung by the force of a shock of self-recognition, of a fleeting intimation of his identity and complicity with Hail-Fellow. In Polanski's variation on the myth, Prince Charming is placed as being of a kind with Hail-Fellow whose taste he carries on his lips; while the beauty whom he would make his princess is presented not as a trophy to be won but as a ticking time bomb. Throughout their time together he fails to perceive that she is mad and that her strangely chill manner and kind of integrity are due to this.

Whether we think of *Knife in the Water* or *Cul de Sac* or *Repulsion*, we may note of Polanski's protagonists that their intransigence and stubborn demeanor shade, to one degree or another, into battiness. Playing things out to a narrower extreme, *Repulsion* offers a refinement and modulation on the types of character and situation found in the two preceding films (and also to be found on a more vulgarized level in *Rosemary's Baby*).

In *Cul de Sac,* hero Donald Pleasance seeks for both himself and a beauty of average price with whom he joins forces (Françoise Dorleac) a free life in a ruined castle by the sea; too normal, however, not to find the scene constraining, the Dorleac character is soon set to go off with the first handy man who passes by. This is one of a series of disasters caused by an intrusion of Hail-Fellows and noise-makers from the ordinary world. He is left at the end of his story—rather like Odysseus at the beginning of his—to weep alone on a rock by the sea. But where the classical hero had sobbed in chagrin and restiveness for a return to the public arena from Calypso's holiday isle, our contemporary figure weeps for the loss of his Calypso to that arena.

Pleasance as opposed to those who disrupt his scene or Deneuve as opposed to those who disrupt hers are similar to the beatnik youth who is set against the average sensual couple in *Knife in the Water*. He joins the couple on their boat for what proves to be a near fatal weekend's sail. The hard-bitten commonplace journalist and his wife, a lush brunette, are comparable to Furneaux and her hard-bitten commonplace boyfriend. In the relationship of either couple, the motive of the woman appears to be more pragmatic than romantic, more a matter of loneliness or other circumstance than of a grand passion. And as Deneuve is made more frenzied by the sound of the nightly set-to's of Furneaux and boyfriend in the room adjoining hers, the beatnik becomes increasingly testy when told of the less than sublime motive—the wish for escape from grimy circumstances—which had led the easy going brunette into marriage with the uptight journalist. For the couple of *Knife in the Water,* the sea marks a holiday element—one which becomes, before their sail is over, a symbol of death, both literal and psychological. The lovers of *Repulsion* take to the sea for a holiday in Italy, only to find waiting for them on their return to their flat a scattered aftermath of lunacy and murder. In each case, the relationship, the "understanding," between the couples is deeply altered through the mania of the protagonist whose own relationship to them approximates that of a competing figure in a love triangle.

The beatnik makes a fuss about his preference for the land, through which he ordinarily wanders with a light pack and heart and switch-blade knife. In contrast to the manner and appearance of the journalist, who is dark, sullen and handy, the beatnik is blond, cool and skittish. In a letter to the *New York Times* which offered some of the best detailed comment on the film I have seen, Dr. Donald J. Marcuse pointed to a shot of the boy slumped on deck "with a coil of rope unmistakably forming a halo behind his head." It is right to see this as a key shot—not, however, as the doctor goes on to do, in order to make heavy Freudian weather of the film as an anthology of "castration and phallic symbols," all there to reinforce an Oedipal scheme. Shots like this one, or like that of the boy climbing the mast, may warrant a Freudian footnote or two, but they serve first a more central and overt dramatic function. *Knife in the Water* is concerned with conflicts and challenges in general between the generations (irrespective of the syndromes of a particular "family romance"). While the fact that the journalist's wife is closer in age to the youth than to her husband does not cancel out a Freudian emphasis, it is fully in keeping with the dramatic. Above all—and subsuming the generation conflict to it—*Knife in the Water* concerns a battle between temperamental types (one which, as it defines itself, shows various points of similarity to the battle lines drawn up by Edward Albee in his *Zoo Story*). To apply a down-the-line Freudian interpretation to the "confrontations" and tensions evoked in the film would be to vitiate and simplify their interest. And since Polanski is as improvisatory and playful a director as Fellini or Godard, the danger of a too sober-sides and schematic approach to his work is that one may easily miss the wit for the complex—the whole spirit of the thing for the random (Freudian) joke. This holds especially for a film like *Repulsion:* to see in it no more than a sensationalist case study in sexual repression, as most critics were content to do, is to miss precisely those ingredients in the film which add to it dimensions over and above such a banal level of interest.[1]

[1] Compare Miss Deneuve's role in *Repulsion*, for example, with her role in *Belle de Jour*, where again she is cast as a type of sexually distraught, "unfulfilled" hysteric. In Bunuel's film, as the restive wife of a medical student, she signs on for a series of afternoon sessions in a brothel as if she were matriculating for an adult education course. This gives us a plot so neatly in contrast with that of *Repulsion* as to be its complement. And a role which Deneuve seems to have been led by the director not so much to perform as to model. The plot itself, which requires her to make frequent changes from one chic costume to another, in boudoir or bordello, also assures the film the box office appeal of a combined fashion-and-strip show.

In *Repulsion*, Deneuve is costumed throughout in the strictest, almost homespun, way. To be sure, her style of dress in each film conforms to that of the character portrayed. And it is in keeping with Bunuel's emphasis on the impersonality of the sex relation by itself that his heroine too should be depersonalized. Yet while exploring the facts of the impersonality of sex with his heroine and leading her and the audience to this not terribly earthshaking discovery, Bunuel also manages a mild send up of the star herself precisely through her "representativeness"—as archetypal bored swinging middle class dummy. In this way he manages to score as well one up on his art house audience—an audience comprised in the main of the cultivated middle class who go to a film like *Belle de Jour* all primed for yet another dose of middle class baiting "shocks" and teasers: especially when these are legitimatized and made easily explicable—as the heroine's antics and visions in this film are—through a scene, planted early, of some traumatic childhood experience.

Thus Deneuve is leveled out to a glamorized mannikin who serves the purposes of a tough-minded object lesson in sex—a lesson completed in a happy ending, no less, as the heroine and her husband are shown facing the new day healthily "liberated" and wealthy and wise. It's all nothing if not medicinal. *Repulsion* dispenses with such pacifying rationalizations; it is a film without a message and with a real terror. Keeping its star in the foreground, it allows her role to attain to a level of mystery. And it exploits surprisingly few box office guarantees.

Bunuel is clearly among the major directors with whom Polanski in fact shares deep affinities. For this reason, too, a comparison with *Belle de Jour*—which happens to be an overrated film, not in a class with Bunuel's best—may help in our appreciation of the younger director's own style and powers. More openly and radically subjective than Bunuel's, his style proves also in this instance to be less indulgent.

But in order to gain a fuller sense of the film, it may be useful to pause further over certain details of the earlier works. Of *Knife in the Water's* trio of characters it is the beatnik—and this is what is pointed up in the shot posing him against a halo of rope—who is given some touch of grace, of spiritual tensity and exuberance. Granted his own capacity for the nasty riposte, his own flaws, he comes over as the freest person on the scene. And after his symbolic and pretended death by drowning (from which he returns to life and a renewal of morale in the wife's arms), he heads off back through the land, still travelling light, while the couple, of the earth the earthiest, remain stuck together in their car, stalled on a muddy road.

The couple themselves define a further contrast which recurs in Polanski's films. If the husband's materialism is immitigably sodden in its manner, that of the wife is near transcendent in its sheer ripeness, in the pathos of its vulnerability, a burden of pathos not the least hidden behind the snappy sunglasses the wife sports. Between the scowling adult and nervy youth, she mediates like an umpire, keeping score and calling fouls; and when finally she takes the youth to her, it is as much a matter of keeping the contest even as of heeding a tide of lust, for the husband had gone so far as to lose his rival's cherished knife in the sea: a foul play waiting to be evened up, as it is by the wife and youth when they embrace to add a capping nuance, as it were, to the metaphor of "knife in the water." The wife's role here adumbrates the more limited and tangential one played by Furneaux in *Repulsion,* who is shown in the opening sequence acting as a mediator between her scowling lover and his opponent, her younger sister.

In *Cul de Sac* it is Donald Pleasance who represents the cry of the maddened spirit *vis-à-vis* the harsh compromises of the mundane world: having given up his business and put his whole stake into his haunt by the sea, he hopes to live there in happy-go-lucky and kinky bliss with his bride. Of those who intrude on his realm, the most sympathetic is his complete opposite, an unillusioned gangster so encumbered and hog-tied in circumstance, so utterly of the earth, that he not only bears the pathos of the earthbound as much as the heroine of *Knife in the Water,* but, as a more extremely drawn variation on this type, is now seen as victim: a snagged victim of the war of romance with reality who, like a Mercutio trapped among the hang-ups of others, unwilling yet stoic before the arbitrariness of his situation, is tagged finally by the random bullet. Throughout, the gangster faces and suffers this fate with a manner of appalled expectation. (In this role Lionel Stander was able triumphantly to sum up the *persona* of his career.) *Cul de Sac* seems to me Polanski's most brilliant film, and among the best of recent years. The linked opposition of types portrayed in it by Pleasance and Stander marks out the dramatic center, the heart and key mood, of Polanski's films from his early short, whose title *The Fat and the Lean* defines the psychic polarities at their center, through his subsequent work. *The Fat and the Lean* is justly famous for the emotional power generated through the wit and play of its surrealistic method. What adds to the interest—and difficulty—of a film like *Repulsion* is the hard-edged naturalistic surface to which both the surreal and the emotional are harnessed and cannily controlled.

We may, then, understand Deneuve in *Repulsion* as a feminine peer and close relation to the knife-bearing youth of *Knife in the Water* and Pleasance's harried recluse in *Cul de Sac*. She is one of Polanski's "lean" types. In contrast we have Furneaux and the giggling co-manicurist who may be seen as distantly related in their role and style to the wife of *Knife in the Water* and the Stander character in *Cul de Sac*. The "lean" central figure of *Repulsion* is one, of course, in whom the spirit has gone wholly berserk, having retreated to a madness of freedom in self-enclosure.

Crisis and turning-point occur when the sister, over Deneuve's protests, defects from their flat for a holiday with boyfriend. To add a taunting spice to misery, the latter forgets about taking his razor from the washstand. Deneuve is thus left astray; and the consequent series of acts she commits to the culminating moment when she reaches for the razor graph a rising arc of horror in a hysterical exacting, at first defiant then defensive, of earth's blood.

The first instance occurs in the beauty salon. An aging customer lies stretched out on a slab awaiting a facial and manicure. She is a caricature of one totally possessed by the social realm, her speech and manner (which recall the style of the family of English burghers whom Polanski sends up with obvious relish in the palace lunch scene of *Cul de Sac*) as dull and palsied as her flesh; of a sudden Deneuve jabs her nail file hard into the woman's thumb, drawing blood and screams.

There is nothing left for Deneuve after this but to incarcerate herself in her flat, where Nice Guy soon hastens, breaking open the door she had boarded up. But she is deep now in the transports of her madness and faces him unheeding and silent as, heedless himself of the enormous danger, he comes on with sincerity and due concern. It is a remarkable scene, equal in the chilling paradoxes of its style and point to Hitchcock: beyond the open door we are given a view of the corridor without where, at the end of its length, we see the hunched and baggy figure of a woman who appears to have stopped on her way out to the street to take in the tensely posed couple in the frame of the door: she stands stock still, a figure of vague curiosity, hazy in outline, essentially indifferent. This shot serves to maintain the identification of Nice Guy with the public world. And when he shuts the door on the corridor and the figure perched there—on his world—he seals his fate: Deneuve raises a candlestick on his turned back and bursts open his head as he had burst open her door. The shock to us, in this smashing of our expectations, is compounded as she keeps at it, striking again and again—even as in the salon she would not stop once she had begun jabbing at her client, or as later, she sustains her attack on another less well-intentioned intruder.

This last is the landlord who had been dunning the sisters for rents overdue. Deneuve has the money for him but, taken not only by her beauty but by the ghostliness and decay of her place—to him as romantic as some haunted ruin come upon in a moonlit wood—he makes a lunge for its tenant to receive for his pains a razor slash on the neck. Holding before him the hand he'd placed to his neck, he stares at the blood on it in unbelief before being slashed to pieces in a further irresistible onslaught.

On the return of Furneaux and boyfriend to the apartment, it is left to the latter to lift up Deneuve—whom they find under her bed, open-eyed and inviolate in her sleep of madness—and carry her past the crowd gathered in the corridor to a waiting ambulance. To boyfriend she had in various ways been a disturbing presence, so it is no surprise that there should be the hint of a smirk on his features as he carries her—in a shot which might in another context be that of a bride being taken over a threshold—out at last into the world and world's claims on her.

The film's method is to keep us aware throughout of—to borrow a phrase from *The Sorrows of Young Werther*—the "inner circumstances" of its protagonist's actions; yet we are offered no explanations, by way of flashback or other means of diagnostic interlude, about the shaping traumas of her character. Polanski neither motivates her psychosis nor seeks to exculpate her behavior in clinical terms. On this score she remains as opaque and unclassifiable as young Werther in his passion for Charlotte. If we respond to the poetry of Goethe's novel or Polanski's film, we respond not to a case history of a sort which allows us to indulge in a patronizing stance or—despite all the wailing in *Werther* and blood-letting in *Repulsion*—to merely sensationalistic kicks but rather to the affecting power with which each artist gets over—as he captures it through sensibilities determined by *amour fou* or outright psychosis —a sense of the blind and terrible passionlessness of the mundane, of the accepted Norm.

Polanski's angle of vision is romantic; it accords in particular with that tendency in Romanticism marked by a devotion to states of being child-like, beleaguered, and far from innocent. As Mary McCarthy has put it, ". . . it is just this state, of the dissociated outsider, that is at the center of our modern literature of sensibility and sensation alike." Both "sensibility and sensation" combine in Polanski's films to give them their unique power. The films place us in such relation to the "inner circumstances" of their wild protagonists as to open up for us perspectives on the everyday scene of an eerie acuity and intransigence.

Miss McCarthy's purpose in her essay on "Characters in Fiction" is to brood on the blind alley—resulting from a narrowing of social interest—to which she feels a literature excessively dependent on such protagonists as saintly mutes, visionary thugs, wan drifters, demonic artists and all the rest of the company of our time's romantic mythology has led. My own purpose in citing her remarks is not at all to worry over why Carson McCullers can't be like Tolstoy or Roman Polanski like Abel Gance or Jean Renoir. It is chiefly to note the integral quality of Polanski's sensibility: analogous to, and with roots in, the cultural context discussed by Miss McCarthy, Polanski's achievement is neither eccentrically "offbeat" nor simply exploitative. It may be that the novel is presently foundering on the problem posed by Miss McCarthy (whose own *The Group,* indeed, what with the limp array of Vassar-honed Millie Lomans who comprise its center, serves to remind of the large odds and handicaps facing the writer who would place mundane reality in an altogether mundane perspective); in films, which provide possibly the medium most suited to it, the new romantic mythology continues to be drawn on to original and compelling effect.

Along with its use of this mythology, the authentically romantic work of our time is recognizable too in being invariably anti-Romantic in theme. *Repulsion* is such a romantically atmospheric anti-Romance. As are, to take a few notable examples, Chabrol's *The Cousins;* Losey's *Eva;* Bunuel's *Viridiana* or his *The Criminal Life of Archibaldo de la Cruz.* The lead figures in works of this kind are not only "dissociated" but also obsessive. It is this conjunction of aloofness with passion (a conjunction which equally defines the style of the films themselves) which gives the characters their charge.

The opening shot of *Repulsion* is on the open shutter of Catherine Deneuve's eye: though brought forward in discomfiting close-up, the eye doesn't look straight at us: rather, its focus is away, beyond us, for the soul whose look it carries is elsewhere, out of our world. The film's closing shot is a closeup on the photograph on Deneuve's bedstand. Earlier, she had had occasion to show it to Nice Guy: it is a picture of herself as a young girl together with her family; again we note that she is not really with the group she stands among, for the film camera singles out her features to reveal that she was not looking in the direction of the camera which took the family portrait; her glance was away, fierce and ominous in its off-centered concentration. Hers is already the eye of a Maenad, an avenging fury.

TARGETS:
An Unshielding Darkness
by BRIAN HENDERSON

Targets, by Peter Bogdanovich, is a film about sniper assassination that is interesting to watch, builds to an exciting if conventional conclusion, and explodes in the mind afterwards with genuine moral significance.

The film tells two stories that come together at the end. One concerns Bobby Thompson, a pleasant-looking young man who kills his wife and mother and goes on a killing spree before he is finally arrested. On the day before his rampage, Bobby adds a high-powered rifle to his large collection of firearms, has supper with his family, and later watches television. The next day he shoots his wife and mother, shoots highway motorists from an oil tank, and shoots members of a drive-in audience from behind the screen. At the drive-in police come and arrest him. The other story, intercut with the first, concerns a group of low-budget film-makers who specialize in horror pictures. Byron Orlok (played by Boris Karloff) is a famous horror film star who announces his intention to retire from films and return to England where he was born. His producers oppose this and so does Sammy (played by Bogdanovich), the young director of Orlok's recent films, who will have to return to television if Orlok retires. As a further complication, Sammy is having an affair with Jenny, Orlok's attractive Chinese secretary. Byron holds to his refusal to make another film, but agrees to make a final appearance, at a drive-in reopening, rather than be sued by his producers. Byron arrives at the drive-in after the film has begun, and

Appeared originally as Targets *in* Film Heritage *4, no. 4 (Summer 1969): 1–8. Copyright © 1969 by F. A. Macklin. Reprinted by permission of* Film Heritage *and the author.*

after some confusion, finds the sniper and disarms him just as the police arrive.

The scenes with the film-makers are enveloped in a thick ambience of cinematic reference. The film begins with the conclusion of a horror film starring Orlok. Lights come up on a projection room and there are garbled voices in the background. This opening is from *Citizen Kane* and the ensuing scene, with producer, director, famous Hollywood face, and attractive script-girl translator, is from *Contempt*. And on and on. At times these scenes seem made up to support the movie jokes and references, as when Sammy wakes up next to Orlok in bed and is, of course, horrified. Sammy's name evokes the hero-villain of *What Makes Sammy Run?* but the reference is ironic for these people are easy-going and likeable, probably the nicest Hollywood characters ever put in a movie. Also, Bogdanovich makes a point of their cultivation. One producer had high honors at Princeton, Jenny has a degree in Chinese from Oxford, and Sammy has done some of his directoral preparation at the Museum of Modern Art, where he saw Howard Hawks' *The Criminal Code* (1931), an excerpt from which is included in the film.

The drive-in finale is the unification of the two plots that the film has hinted at from its beginning. But we still wonder why the two stories have been brought together in the first place. We go through several half-formed conceptions—that horror films lead to violence, that real horror is different from film horror—until we come to the right one: The film-makers have failed to nourish their audience. They have not provided an imaginative environment to overcome the sterile environment in which the Thompsons live, or to have led to a different environment. Bobby has starved in this environment: he has failed to become a person. His good clothes and new car are deceptive, Bobby is as cut off from the wherewithal to become fully human as any character in Zola or James T. Farrell.

Throughout the film the film-makers are oblivious of any connection with their audience. They are gentle in manner but so drenched with self-concern that they cannot see beyond themselves. Byron refers to a newspaper story about a multiple shooting in a supermarket to make the point that his kind of horror is obsolete, and Sammy agrees. On his way to the drive-in Byron looks at block after block of desolate used car lots and remarks sadly that the city has changed. He thinks not of those who live in this emptiness but of the tedium of the landscape as he passes through. The film-

makers view American life as a sad spectacle in no way connected
with themselves. The real nature of that connection is revealed by
the excerpt from *The Criminal Code.* In the excerpted scene, Boris
Karloff as a prison guard or trustee approaches and kills a doomed
prisoner, trapped like a rat, in the midst of a prison riot. At the
end of *Targets,* Karloff as Orlok approaches and disarms Bobby in
much the same way. This parallelism suggests that Bobby's shooting
spree has been like an aimless prison riot that has succeeded only in
killing some of his fellow prisoners and himself. It suggests also
that the film-makers are no better than prison guards in their relation to the public.

The connection between the two stories is greatest in the film's
cumulative effect. The parallel stories are a kind of moral balance
sheet, or statement of charges, but the bill is not presented until
after the end. Two factors put us off the track, serving not only to
postpone the film's judgment but to obscure the processes of judgment as they are carefully built up. One is the atmosphere of
cinematic lore. Because of this element we do not take the filmmaker scenes seriously. We sit back and enjoy them or are irritated
by them, but—we sit back. We lower our guard. The other factor is
that the poverty in which the Thompsons live is not economic. The
film is not a study of have and have not in the conventional sense.
The Thompsons are not poor, the film-makers are not rich. In
dollars and cents the two sets of characters are about equal; but
that is the old way of figuring. The film-makers are sophisticated
international citizens; they know what is good in the world. More
importantly, each of them is a fully-developed person. (Though
we see finally that Bobby and his fate are a limit on their personage.
So long as he is not free, they cannot be free.) We even feel, because
of the equality of wealth, that each group has chosen to live as it
does. But this is wrong. It is one of the walls that crumble about
us when we begin to put the two stories together. Bobby has never
chosen, has never had a choice. This is a failure of imagination,
for it is the power and function of imagination to reveal choices,
to raise up options where there was only necessity. The film-makers,
as tutors of the public imagination, share seriously in the blame for
this failure.

Thus we do not see the relation between the two stories though
Bogdanovich develops that relation from the beginning of the film.
He does this by juxtaposing the two sets of characters as he cuts

back and forth between them, developing contrasts in character
and in environment.

At first we are prepared to be as interested in Bobby as in the
film people. The latter are too comfortable and self-absorbed. Orlok
is kindly, but Sammy is peevish and rather selfish. Jenny is indeter-
minate, somewhere between them in this as she is in the plot-work.
But as the film progresses we become involved with the film-makers,
come to like them quite a bit, and Bobby can't keep pace. We
realize fairly soon: there is only one dimension to his personality.
He interests us only as a murderer. The director's cleverness here is
to occupy us with one process, getting to like Sammy and the others,
while a larger process, absorption of the whole film and its import,
slowly and silently takes place.

The contrast in environment/decor is more fully realized. Scenes
with the film-makers are shot almost entirely against warm and
sheltering interiors: a snug projection room, Orlok's elegant, out-
dated hotel suite, a dim restaurant table, the protective inside of the
limousine which takes Orlok and Jenny to the drive-in. The one time
they appear on the street in daylight, caught between studio and
waiting car, they seem to bring the sheltering dimness of projection
room and hotel suite with them. These interiors, warm and intimate
when light, rich and mellow when dark, have a modest elegance but
not opulence. We are never dazzled, we are comfortably at home.
Colors in these scenes are also deep and rich: Orlok's gray and
brown tweeds and tanned skin, Sammy's vivid yellow sweater,
Jenny's smart outfits, Orlok's black tuxedo against auto interiors
and against the night.

The Thompsons, on the other hand, live their lives in the open;
indoors and outdoors they are at the mercy of a fierce and penetrating light. The first time we see Bobby he goes into a gun shop from
the sunny street: we feel there is nowhere else he can go for shelter
and relief. At home he walks the living room in silence but the
voices of his mother and wife cut through the walls, which seem
paper thin. There is no shelter for him anywhere. The rooms of the
house, painted in thin pastels, are filled with an empty, brittle light,
not a corner escapes the functional brightness. Even the darkness is
unshielding. At one point Orlok puts out the light in his hotel
room; after an interval a match is struck and we see Bobby smoking
a cigarette in bed. The very quality of the two darknesses is different, Orlok's warm and rich, Bobby's cold and thin. The scenes
with the Thompsons are painful—cold and hurtful to the eye and

to the tactile sense. This deprivation is softened for us by the alternating warm scenes with the film people. Then we realize that
Bobby must spend his life in that open, under that merciless banal
light, and we see the trap he is in.

Bogdanovich's skill in juxtaposing the two environments and the
emotional flavor of each is demonstrated by the fact that we are not
aware of a juxtaposition at all until after the film. Only then do
we realize the extent to which our emotions have been influenced by
the purely visual element of the film. (Compare Richard Brooks'
In Cold Blood where the inter-story contrast, as in the cut from
Perry shaving in a men's room to Mr. Clutter shaving comfortably
at home, is not only noticeable but obtrusive. It takes skill not to be
ironic when irony is implicit in the material.)

The nature of Bobby's environment has a further implication.
There is no attempt in the film to differentiate Bobby from millions
of people who live as he does. There is no psychoanalytic explanation for his behavior. (*Repulsion* is an interesting comparison.) The
cause of Bobby's murders is the totality of his environment. Most
reviewers noted this feature of the film but did not consider it in
the context of the film's double story. Our judgment that the
American environment is sterile might be enough if the film presented only Bobby and his actions. But Bogdanovich includes our
viewpoint in the film, in the cultivated presence of the film-makers,
and lays it up against the spectacle of Bobby and his actions. We
are to relate the two, see if our posture toward it has anything to
do with the spectacle itself. It is interesting that most critics con-
centrated on the story of Bobby and wrote as if the film-makers were
invisible.

The final sequence of *Targets* may be taken as an image of American life: creative America meets mass America at the drive-in. It is
built up by cutting among five situations: the projection booth of
the drive-in, run by a single old man; the sniper in position behind
the screen, technicolor light playing on his face through a hole he
has made for his rifle; the patrons of the drive-in massed in rows of
cars in front of the screen; the screen itself, showing the Byron
Orlok picture which began the film; and Orlok, Jenny, and Sammy,
shown on their way and later arriving at the drive-in, unaware of
what is happening. After it is dark and the picture has begun,
Bobby begins shooting at persons in a row of cars somewhere in

front of him. His victims are close together, no more than six feet apart, but cut off from one another. Each family, sealed in its automobile, is unaware that people to the right and left are being murdered. Sound units turned up, eyes fixed upon the screen, they cannot hear cries for help nor see the agony of their neighbors. Warning is given with difficulty; the attention of the neighbor must be attracted, his sound unit turned off, his window rolled down. Leaving one's car to rap on another's window is very dangerous because one's inside light goes on when the door is opened. One man loses his life this way.

Bobby shoots the projectionist also, who throws a switch starting up the next reel before he dies. As this reel runs down Bogdanovich cuts repeatedly to the emptying spool, giving it a dramatic interest equal to that of the other situations. This seems a perverse cineaste joke—only a film-lover regards the sputtering end of a spool as a poignant event under any circumstances—but it has dramatic justification. If the film ran out, the viewers would protest for a while and then go home; also, with the sound gone they would hear the shooting and cries for help. It is the movie which keeps them in the danger zone. The film image has them in a trance: until the spell is broken no help may be asked or given and no news of common perils passed. The image isolates the viewers at the same time that it masses them: a vivid suggestion of the effect of all media.

The film-makers come late and the projectionist lies dead: Who takes responsibility for this image and its effects? The film runs on, it is attended carefully, it does its destructive work, but there is no one behind it. Its viewers recall the man in Kafka who is sent news from a dead emperor and, possibly, revelation from a God who has departed the world. In *Targets* it is human gods who have abandoned their creation. Those who control public media have put their messages in operation and absented themselves, taking no interest in the effects of their handiwork. The unmanned projector, rattling on autonomously, is a vivid image of anarchy and chaos, like the baby carriage rolling down the steps in *Potemkin*. The pairing of god-like power with only human responsibility issues in violence and destruction.

Some have criticized the junction of the two plots in the drive-in sequence as contrived and melodramatic. Of course this ending is melodramatic, but it is a "movie" way of affirming a moral relationship between the two sets of characters. The movie points to the world in this way, in the only way it can, in terms of the signs and strategies that constitute it as an art-form. This is true not just of the ending but of the entire film: *Targets* not only comments on horror films, it is itself a horror film and follows the rules of the genre. Bobby is a kind of monster whom Orlok, himself usually a monster, in the end subdues. In a real sense, by implication of the film, Orlok has created this monster. His enigmatic words after he has disarmed Bobby, "I was afraid of this," remind us of those uttered by movie scientists after their creations have been brought to ruin. The stages of *Targets,* creation and escape of a monster, destruction caused by the monster, final subduing of the monster, and its narrative technique, intercutting between two situations, are those of the classical horror film.

Like other modern artists, Bogdanovich takes liberties with his genre, subverts it, inverts it, runs it against itself, at the same time as he proceeds in terms of it. His film undermines the form and criticizes the culture which produced it, but it recognizes itself in that culture. Bogdanovich's use of the horror film genre acknowledges the inescapable shaping influence of that culture upon him, as well as his involvement in it. Perhaps to work in it is the way to work out of it.

The moral trajectory of *Targets* is described in a "scary story" which Orlok recites at a run-through for his drive-in appearance that evening. It is Somerset Maugham's brief tale, used as epigraph for John O'Hara's *Appointment In Samarra,* of the servant who brushes Death in the marketplace at Bagdad and flees to Samarra to escape her. Death herself, speaking to the servant's master, says that she was surprised to see the servant in Bagdad, for she had an appointment with him that night in Samarra. The story has an obvious plot reference: Orlok, seeking to escape a lawsuit, goes to the drive-in where, in fact, a greater threat awaits him. Orlok does not die at the drive-in, but he meets a moral fate there. His planned retirement to England is an attempt to escape his work in America but, in his last appearance there, that work catches up with him in the person of Bobby. His words "I was afraid of this" and his sad turning away suggest that he has realized his relation to Bobby. More generally, all the film-makers have been involved in a journey of escape from responsibility, and for all of them the events at the drive-in are an overtaking by fate.

For several critics, Bogdanovich's "implication" of the audience in the sniper's act of shooting is the moral point of the film. When he lines up his shot, one reviewer said, we do not want him to miss. Whether this is true or not, the important thing is that we would never do what Bobby does. Once in place and set up we too might pull the trigger. The difference is that we would not take even the first step to get in that position. It is, if anything, our comfortable distance from what Bobby does, our remoteness from his desperation, which implicates us. In this sense the figure of flight and overtaking fits, in its most general application: the outermost of three concentrics, the experience of the viewer as well. By our identification with the film-makers and the warmth of their environment, we too have sought to escape connection with Bobby and his environment; and we too are overtaken in that the moral energies of the film are directed against the film-makers rather than the Thompsons. In this light the film-buff trappings serve an insidious purpose also; they operate to implicate us in the self-love and self-absorption of the film-makers. Seemingly digressive, they lead, like the servant's flight from Bagdad, straight to the heart of judgment.

Lastly, though it smacks of college English, the name of the pivotal character of the film is a clue to its meaning. Byron Orlok: Byron or Locke, two kinds of individualism, two modes of American life. One of these is the Byronic individualism of the film-makers and of much of the American intellectual and artistic community generally: indifference to "the crowd." The aloofness of the film-makers is exhibited not in their words but in their actions and in their work. The poet's words "I stood/Among them, but not of them" sum up fairly well their relation to the Thompsons and people like them; this is explicit where Byron sits among the crowd at the drive-in in his limousine.

"The crowd" itself represents the flowering of Lockean social and political individualism. Distrustful of their neighbors they buy and keep guns; distrustful of government they deny it, among other things, the power to regulate firearms. Above all, distrustful of community and community values they live and take their pleasures in a needless isolation. This impoverishes their lives and cuts them off from effective communal action which might change their situation.

That these defective individualisms are correlative, that they reinforce each other, is the burden of *Targets*.

Filmography[1]

1908

Dr. Jekyll and Mr. Hyde. USA (Selig Polyscope).

1910

Dr. Jekyll and Mr. Hyde. Denmark (Nordisk).
Frankenstein. USA (Edison Co.).

1912

The Conquest of the Pole. France (Star Films). D: Georges Méliès.
Dr. Jekyll and Mr. Hyde. USA (Thanhauser).

1913

Dr. Jekyll and Mr. Hyde. Great Britain (Kineto-Kinemacolor).
Dr. Jekyll and Mr. Hyde. USA (IMP).
The Student of Prague. Germany (Bioscope).

1914

The Avenging Conscience. USA (Mutual). D: D. W. Griffith; PA: Blanche Sweet, Mae Marsh.
The Golem. Germany (Bioscope). D: Paul Wegener, Henrik Galeen.

1915

Life without Soul. USA (Ocean Film Corp.). Adapted from Mary Shelley's *Frankenstein.*

[1] The following symbols are used throughout: D=director; P=producer; S=scriptwriter; M=music composer; PA=principal actor(s) or actress(es).

1916

Homunculus. German (Bioscope).

1919

The Cabinet of Dr. Caligari. Germany (Decla-Bioscope). D: Robert Wiene;
PA: Conrad Veidt, Werner Krauss.
The Ghost of Slumber Mountain. USA (World-Cinema Distributing Co.).
Special effects: Willis O'Brien.

1920

Dr. Jekyll and Mr. Hyde. USA (Pioneer Film Corp.). P: Louis B. Mayer.
Dr. Jekyll and Mr. Hyde. USA (Paramount). PA: John Barrymore.
The Golem. Germany (UFA). D: Paul Wegener, Carl Boese; Photographer:
Karl Freund.

1921

The Haunted Castle. Germany (Decla-Bioscope). D: F. W. Murnau; S:
Carl Mayer, Berthold Viertel.
Witchcraft Through the Ages. Sweden (Svenska).

1922

Nosferatu. Germany (Prana Co.). D: F. W. Murnau; PA: Max Schreck.

1924

Waxworks. Germany (Neptun-Films). D: Paul Leni; PA: Emil Jannings,
Conrad Veidt, Werner Krauss.

1925

The Hands of Orlac. Austria (Pan-Film). D: Robert Wiene.
The Phantom of the Opera. USA (Universal). P: Carl Laemmle; PA: Lon
Chaney.

1926

The Bat. USA (United Artists).
The Bells. USA (Chadwick). PA: Lionel Barrymore, Boris Karloff.
The Student of Prague. Germany (Sokal). PA: Conrad Veidt, Werner Krauss.

1927

London After Midnight. USA (M-G-M). D: Tod Browning; PA: Lon Chaney.
The Unknown. USA (M-G-M). D: Tod Browning; PA: Lon Chaney, Joan Crawford.

1928

House of Horror. USA (First National).
The Terror. USA (Warner Bros.).

1929

The Thirteenth Chair. USA (M-G-M). D: Tod Browning; PA: Conrad Nagel, Bela Lugosi.

1930

The Bat Whispers. USA (United Artists).

1931

Dracula. USA (Universal). D: Tod Browning; Photographer: Karl Freund; PA: Bela Lugosi.
Frankenstein. USA (Universal). D: James Whale; PA: Boris Karloff.

1932

Dr. Jekyll and Mr. Hyde. USA (Paramount). D: Rouben Mamoulian; PA: Frederic March, Miriam Hopkins.
Dr. X. USA (First National/Warner). D: Michael Curtiz; PA: Lionel Atwill, Fay Wray.

Freaks. USA (M-G-M). D: Tod Browning.

Island of Lost Souls. USA (Paramount). D: Erle C. Kenton; PA: Charles Laughton, Bela Lugosi.

The Mummy. USA (Universal). D: Karl Freund; PA: Boris Karloff.

Murders in the Rue Morgue. USA (Universal). D: Robert Florey; Photographer: Karl Freund; PA: Bela Lugosi.

The Old Dark House. USA (Universal). D: James Whale; PA: Boris Karloff.

Vampyr. France (Les Films Carl Dreyer). D: Carl Dreyer; Photographer: Rudolf Maté.

The White Zombie. USA (Amusement Securities). PA: Bela Lugosi.

1933

The Ghoul. Great Britain (Gaumont British). PA: Boris Karloff.

The Invisible Man. USA (Universal). D: James Whale; PA: Claude Rains.

King Kong. USA (RKO Radio). D: Merian C. Cooper, Ernest B. Schoedsack; Special effects: Willis O'Brien: PA: Fay Wray, Robert Armstrong, Bruce Cabot.

Mystery of the Wax Museum. USA (Warner Bros.). D: Michael Curtiz; PA: Lionel Atwill.

Son of Kong. USA (RKO Radio). D: Ernest B. Schoedsack; Special effects: Willis O'Brien.

The Vampire Bat. USA (Majestic). PA: Lionel Atwill.

1934

The Black Cat. USA (Universal). PA: Bela Lugosi, Boris Karloff.

1935

The Bride of Frankenstein. USA (Universal). D: James Whale; M: Franz Waxman; PA: Boris Karloff, Elsa Lanchester.

The Mark of the Vampire. USA (M-G-M). D: Tod Browning; PA: Bela Lugosi, Lionel Atwill.

The Raven. USA (Universal). PA: Boris Karloff, Bela Lugosi.

1936

The Devil Doll. USA (M-G-M). D: Tod Browning.

Dracula's Daughter. USA (Universal). PA: Bela Lugosi, Gloria Holden.

The Invisible Ray. USA (Universal). PA: Boris Karloff, Bela Lugosi.

The Walking Dead. USA (Warner Bros.). D: Michael Curtiz; PA: Boris Karloff.

1939

The Hound of the Baskervilles. USA (20th Century-Fox). PA: Basil Rathbone.

Son of Frankenstein. USA (Universal). PA: Basil Rathbone, Boris Karloff, Bela Lugosi, Lionel Atwill.

1940

Dr. Cyclops. USA (Paramount). D: Ernest B. Schoedsack.
The Mummy's Hand. USA (Universal).

1941

The Black Cat. USA (Universal). PA: Basil Rathbone, Bela Lugosi.
Dr. Jekyll and Mr. Hyde. USA (M-G-M). D: Victor Fleming; M: Franz Waxman; PA: Spencer Tracy, Ingrid Bergman.
The Wolf Man. USA (Universal). PA: Bela Lugosi. Lon Chaney, Jr.

1942

The Cat People. USA (RKO-Radio). P: Val Lewton; D: Jacques Tourneur; PA: Simone Simon.
The Ghost of Frankenstein. USA (Universal). PA: Lon Chaney, Jr., Bela Lugosi, Lionel Atwill.
The Mummy's Tomb. USA (Universal). PA: Lon Chaney, Jr.

1943

Frankenstein Meets the Wolf Man. USA (Universal). PA: Lon Chaney, Jr., Bela Lugosi.
I Walked with a Zombie. USA (RKO-Radio). P: Val Lewton; D: Jacques Tourneur.
The Phantom of the Opera. USA (Universal). PA: Nelson Eddy, Susanna Foster, Claude Rains.
Son of Dracula. USA (Universal). PA: Lon Chaney, Jr.

1944

The Curse of the Cat People. USA (RKO-Radio). P: Val Lewton.

House of Frankenstein. USA (Universal). PA: Boris Karloff, Lon Chaney, Jr.

The Lodger. USA (20th Century-Fox). Photographer: Lucien Ballard; PA: Laird Cregar.

The Mummy's Curse. USA (Universal). PA: Lon Chaney, Jr.

The Mummy's Ghost. USA (Universal). PA: Lon Chaney, Jr.

The Return of the Vampire. USA (Columbia). PA: Bela Lugosi.

The Uninvited. USA (Paramount). PA: Ray Milland, Ruth Hussey.

1945

The Body Snatcher. USA (RKO-Radio). P: Val Lewton; PA: Boris Karloff, Bela Lugosi.

Dead of Night. Great Britain (Ealing).

House of Dracula. USA (Universal). PA: Lon Chaney, Jr., John Carradine, Lionel Atwill.

Isle of the Dead. USA (RKO-Radio). P: Val Lewton; PA: Boris Karloff.

1946

Bedlam. USA (RKO-Radio). P: Val Lewton; PA: Boris Karloff.

1947

The Beast with Five Fingers. USA (Warner Bros.). D: Robert Florey; PA: Peter Lorre, J. Carrol Naish.

1953

The Beast from 20,000 Fathoms. USA (Warner Bros.).

House of Wax. USA (Warner Bros.). (in 3-D).

The Magnetic Monster. USA (United Artists/Ivan Tors).

1954

Creature From the Black Lagoon. USA (Universal). (in 3-D).

Phantom of the Rue Morgue. USA (Warner Bros.).

1955

Les Diaboliques. France (United Nations Picture Co.). D: H. G. Clouzot.

Godzilla. Japan (Toho).

1956

The Invasion of the Body Snatchers. USA (Allied Artists).

1957

Blood of Dracula. USA (American International).
Curse of the Demon. Great Britain (Sabre/Columbia). D: Jacques Tourneur.
The Curse of Frankenstein. Great Britain (Hammer Films). D: Terence Fisher; PA: Peter Cushing, Christopher Lee.
The Incredible Shrinking Man. USA (Universal).

1958

The Fly. USA (20th Century-Fox). PA: Vincent Price, Herbert Marshall.
Frankenstein 1970. Great Britain (Allied Pictures). PA: Boris Karloff.
Frankenstein's Daughter. USA (Marc Frederick).
Horror of Dracula. Great Britain (Hammer Films). D: Terence Fisher.
The Revenge of Frankenstein. Great Britain (Hammer Films). D: Terence Fisher; PA: Christopher Lee.

1959

Bucket of Blood. USA (Alta Vista/American International). D: Roger Corman.
Horrors of the Black Museum. Great Britain (Anglo Amalgamated).
The Hound of the Baskervilles. Great Britain (Hammer Films). D: Terence Fisher; PA: Peter Cushing, Christopher Lee.
The Mummy. Great Britain (Hammer Films). D: Terrence Fisher.
The Return of the Fly. USA (Associated Producers). PA: Vincent Price.

1960

Black Sunday. Italy (Galatea-Jolly Films). D: Mario Bava; PA: Barbara Steele.
The Brides of Dracula. Great Britain (Hammer Films). D: Terence Fisher; PA: Peter Cushing.
Blood and Roses. France/Italy (Films E.G.E./Documento Films). D: Roger Vadim.

Eyes without a Face, or The Horror Chamber of Dr. Faustus. France/ Italy (Champs-Elysées/Lux). D: Georges Franju; PA: Pierre Brasseur, Alida Valli.

The House of Usher. USA (Alta Vista/American–International). D: Roger Corman; PA: Vincent Price.

Psycho. USA (Shamley/Paramount). D: Alfred Hitchcock; PA: Anthony Perkins, Janet Leigh.

The Village of the Damned. Great Britain (M-G-M).

1961

The Curse of the Werewolf. Great Britain (Hammer Films). D: Terence Fisher.

The Pit and the Pendulum. USA (Alta Vista/American-International). D-P: Roger Corman; PA: Vincent Price, Barbara Steele.

These Are the Damned. Great Britain (Hammer Films/Swallow). D: Joseph Losey.

1962

The Phantom of the Opera. Great Britain (Hammer Films). D: Terence Fisher.

Tales of Terror. USA (American-International). D-P: Roger Corman; PA: Vincent Price, Peter Lorre, Basil Rathbone.

What Ever Happened to Baby Jane? USA (Seven Arts/Aldrich). P-D: Robert Aldrich; PA: Bette Davis, Joan Crawford.

1963

The Birds. USA (Universal). D: Alfred Hitchcock; S: Evan Hunter; PA: Rod Taylor, Tippi Hendren.

Black Sabbath. Italy/France (Emmepi/Galatea/Lyre). D: Mario Bava; PA: Boris Karloff.

The Haunted Palace. USA (Alta Vista/American–International). P-D: Roger Corman; PA: Vincent Price, Lon Chaney, Jr.

The Haunting. Great Britain (Argyle-MGM). P-D: Robert Wise; PA: Julie Harris, Claire Bloom.

The Man with the X-ray Eyes. USA (American-International). D-P: Roger Corman; PA: Ray Milland.

1964

The Curse of the Mummy's Tomb. Great Britain (Hammer/Swallow Films).

The Evil of Frankenstein. Great Britain (Hammer Films). PA: Peter Cushing.

1965

The Curse of the Fly. Great Britain (Lippert Films). PA: Brian Donlevy.
Die, Die, My Darling. Great Britain (Seven Arts/Hammer Films). PA: Tallulah Bankhead.
Dracula, Prince of Darkness. Great Britain (Hammer Films). D: Terence Fisher; PA: Christopher Lee.
Onibaba (*The Hole*). Japan (Toho). D: Kaneto Shindo.
Repulsion. Great Britain (Compton/Tekli). D-S: Roman Polanski; PA: Catherine Deneuve.

1966

Frankenstein Created Woman. Great Britain (Hammer Films). D: Terence Fisher; PA: Peter Cushing.
Plague of the Zombies. Great Britain (Hammer Films).
The Sorcerers. USA (Allied Artists). D: Michael Reeves; PA: Boris Karloff.
The Theatre of Death. Great Britain (Pennea). PA: Christopher Lee.

1967

The Mummy's Shroud. Great Britain (Hammer Films).

1968

Dracula Has Risen From the Grave. Great Britain (Hammer Films). PA: Christopher Lee.
Night of the Living Dead. USA (Reade).
Rosemary's Baby. USA (Paramount). D: Roman Polanski; PA: Mia Farrow, Ruth Gordon, John Cassavetes.
Targets. USA (Paramount). D: Peter Bogdanovich; PA: Boris Karloff.
Witchfinder General. USA (Tigon). D: Michael Reeves.

1969

Fear Chamber. Mexico (Azteca-Columbia). PA: Boris Karloff.
Frankenstein Must Be Destroyed. Great Britain (Warner Bros.). D: Terence Fisher; PA: Peter Cushing.
House of Evil. Mexico (Azteca-Columbia). PA: Boris Karloff.

1971

Cat o' Nine Tails. Italy (National General). PA: Karl Malden, James Franciscus.

Daughters of Darkness. Belgium (Gemini). PA: Delphine Seyrig.

I, Monster. Great Britain (Hammer Films). D: Stephen Weeks; PA: Peter Cushing, Christopher Lee. Adaptation of *Dr. Jekyll and Mr. Hyde.*

Vampire Doll. Japan (Toho). D: Michio Yamamoto.

Bibliography[1]

BOOKS

Ackerman, Forrest J., *The Best From Famous Monsters of Filmland*. New York: Paperback Library, Inc., 1964. A pleasant pictorial survey.

————, *The Frankenscience Monster*. New York: Ace Publishing Corp., 1969. A collection of reminiscences in tribute to the late Boris Karloff.

Boullet, Jean, *La Belle et la Bête*. Paris: le Terrain Vague, 1958. Traces the "beauty and the beast" theme in films, with references to art and literature. Interesting section on *King Kong*.

Butler, Ivan, *The Horror Film*. Cranbury, N.J.: A. S. Barnes & Co., 1967. Historically oriented study of horror as an aspect of certain films rather than as a genre in its own right.

Clarens, Carlos, *An Illustrated History of the Horror Film*. New York: Capricorn Books, 1967. The most complete survey of the genre to date. Well illustrated, with an extensive filmography.

Drake, Douglas, *Horror*. New York: Macmillan, 1966. Interesting attempt to recreate the feeling for horror literature and horror films through atmospheric writing. Some factual errors, however.

Eissner, Lotte, *The Haunted Screen*. Berkeley: The University of California Press,1969. Mainly interested in German expressionism, touching tangentially but brilliantly on the pictorial effects of horror films such as *Nosferatu*.

Everson, William K., *The Bad Guys: A Pictorial History of the Movie Villain*. New York: The Citadel Press, 1964. Contains a useful chapter on monsters.

Gifford, Denis, *Movie Monsters*. New York: E. P. Dutton & Co., Inc., 1969. Slick and well illustrated, each chapter being devoted to a different breed of monster.

Gow, Gordon, *Suspense in the Cinema*. Cranbury, N.J.: A. S. Barnes & Co., 1968. Profusely illustrated account of suspenseful films, of which horror is treated as a subgenre.

Kyrou, Ado, *Le Surrealisme au Cinéma*. Paris: Editions Arcanes, 1953. A competent treatment of a very special aspect of horror.

[1] Items preceded by an asterisk are reprinted in whole or in part in the present volume.

Laclos, Michel, *Le Fantastique au Cinéma*. Paris: J. J. Pauvert, 1958. A classic work, dealing with horror as a sub species of fantasy.

Manchel, Frank, *Terrors of the Screen*. Englewood Cliffs, N.J.: Prentice-Hall, Inc., 1970. Entertaining, anecdotal, and profusely illustrated.

ARTICLES

* Alloway, Lawrence, "Monster Films," *Encounter*, XIV (January, 1960), 70–72. A pictorially and iconographically sensitive account of the monster genre.

Amis, Kingsley, "Dracula, Frankenstein, Son and Co.," in *Whatever Became of Jane Austen?* London: Jonathan Cape, Ltd., 1970. On horror versus science fiction.

* Belz, Carl, "The Birds," *Film Culture*, No. 31 (Winter, 1963–64); 51–53. A consideration of Hitchcock's film as part of the surrealistic movement in art. Published here as "The Terror of the Surreal."

Bogdanovich, Peter, "On *The Birds*," *Film Culture*, No. 28 (Spring, 1963), 69–70. The emphasis is on the symbolism of the birds and on character relationships.

* Bradbury, Ray, "A New Ending to *Rosemary's Baby*," *Films and Filming*, August, 1969, p. 10. An alternate, more demonic-religious ending, suggested by a master of science fiction-fantasy.

Brustein, Robert, "Film Chronicles: Reflections on Horror Movies," *Partisan Review*, XXV (Spring, 1958), 288–96. A standard though superficial account, frequently anthologized.

* Denne, John D., "Society and the Monster," *December*, No. 10, 180–183. An interesting classification of monster films according to the way in which they mirror social conflict.

* Dillard, R. H. W., "Even a Man Who Is Pure at Heart," in W. R. Robinson, ed., *Man and the Movies* (Baton Rouge: Louisiana State University Press, 1967). A well-written discussion of the moral and psychological implications of the genre by a poet and horror film scenarist. Published here as "The Pageantry of Death."

Durgnat, Raymond, "From Pleasure Palace to Libido Motel," *Films and Filming*, VIII (January, 1962), 15, 41, 46. Encompasses the musical spectacular and the psychological thriller, ending with *Psycho*.

———, "Scream Louder, Live Longer: An Introduction to Screen Violence," *The Listener*, LXXII, No. 1862 (December 3, 1964), 880–882. On the cathartic value of horror and terror.

———, "The 'Yellow Peril' Rides Again," *Film Society Review*, V (October, 1969), 36–41. On *The Mask of Fu Manchu* and related horror sagas of the thirties set in the Orient.

* ———, "Les Yeux Sans Visage," in *Franju* (Berkeley: University of California Press, 1967). An uncovering of the subtle devices used by Franju to produce suspense and terror.

Everson, William K., "A Family Tree of Monsters," *Film Culture*, I (January, 1955), 24–30. Detailed account of the "evolution" of standard monsters in the sequels that followed their first appearance.

————, "Horror Films," *Films in Review*, V (January, 1954), 12–23. A solid, entertaining rundown of the development of the genre through the mid-fifties.

* Farber, Stephen, "The New American Gothic," *Film Quarterly*, XX, No. 1 (Fall, 1966), 22–27. The newer films in the Gothic mode seen as visual distortions of reality.

* Farber, Manny, "Val Lewton, 1951," in *Negative Space* (New York: Praeger Publishing Co., 1971), pp. 47–50. An analytical tribute to a master producer of low-budget horror classics. Published here as "Val Lewton and the School of Shudders."

Fisher, Terence, "Horror Is My Business," *Films and Filming*, X (July, 1964), 7–8. A pragmatic view of the problems of production by a director firmly committed to the horror genre.

Glazebrook, Phillip, "The Anti-Heroes of Horror," *Films and Filming*, XIII (October, 1966). A discussion of the audience's identification with the monster-villain.

Grotjahn, Martin, "Horror—Yes, It Can Do You Good," *Films and Filming*, V (November, 1958). A psychiatrist's view of the therapeutic value of the horror film as a controlled nightmare.

Halliwell, Leslie, "The Baron, the Count, and Their Ghoul Friends," *Films and Filming*, XV (June, 1969), 12–16; (July 1969), 13–16. A rather anecdotal survey of certificate ratings for horror films and of the nostalgia for the films themselves.

* Harrington, Curtis, "Ghoulies and Ghosties," *Sight and Sound*, XXI (April–June, 1952), 157–61. An appreciation of contrasting elements from the standpoint of a film director.

* Henderson, Brian, "Targets," *Film Heritage*, IV, No. 4 (Summer, 1969), 1–8. An analysis of the film-within-the-film's horror and suspense effects.

Hill, Derek, "The Face of Horror," *Sight and Sound*, XXVIII (Winter, 1958–59), 6–11. A treatment of the genre as a mirror of the social environment.

Hoda, F., "Epouvante et Science-Fiction," *Positif*, No. 12 (November–December, 1954), 1–17. Traces the evolution of the horror and science fiction genres in America.

Hoveyda, Fereydoun, "Les Grimaces du Demon," *Cahiers du Cinema*, XX (May, 1961), 48–57. Compares the horror genre with science fiction, spiced with references to Freud.

Jensen, Paul, "Frankenstein," *Film Comment*, VI (Fall, 1970). A perceptive account of James Whale's visual style, as well as of the film's plot and performances.

Kane, Joe, "Nuclear Films," *Take One*, II, 9–10. A study of the relation of monster films to the atom bomb.

Karloff, Boris, "My Life as a Monster," *Films and Filming*, IV (November,

1957). The most celebrated player of monsters interprets the meaning of the role.

* Kennedy, X. J., "Who Killed King Kong?" *Dissent,* Spring, 1960. A poet's view of poetic and unpoetic justice in *King Kong.*

Kinder, Marsha, and Beverle Houston, "Rosemary's Baby," *Sight and Sound,* XXXVIII (Winter, 1968–69), 17–19. A sensitive appreciation relying primarily on the film's thematic use of color and other visual effects.

* McConnell, Frank, "Rough Beast Slouching," *Kenyon Review,* No. 1 (1970), 109–20. On the cultural relevance of the horror genre.

* Ollier, Claude, "Un Roi à New York," *Cahiers du Cinéma,* No. 166–67 (May–June, 1965), 65–72. A detailed analysis of the plot construction, pictorial effects, and socioeconomic themes in *King Kong.*

Oudart, Jean-Pierre, "Humain, Trop Humain," *Cahiers du Cinéma,* No. 210 (March, 1969), 57–58. A perceptive essay on Browning's *Freaks.*

Pechter, William S., "The Director Vanishes," *Moviegoer,* No. 2 (Summer–Autumn, 1964), 37–50. A good rundown on the career of Hitchcock, with an especially fine section on *The Birds.*

* Perez, Michel, "Le Désespoir Puritan," *Positif,* No. 92 (February, 1968), 61–63. A culturally oriented account of the imagery and form of *I Walked with a Zombie.*

* ———, "Le Cinéma Retrouvé: *Dr. Jekyll and Mr. Hyde,*" *Positif,* No. 76 (June, 1966), 130–134. A comparison of the Fleming version of the story with others, most notably with Mamoulian's.

Pirie, David, "New Blood," *Sight and Sound,* Spring, 1971, pp. 73–75. A discussion of the younger British directors concentrating on the horror film.

* Ross, T. J., "Roman Polanski, *Repulsion,* and the New Mythology," *Film Heritage,* IV (Winter, 1968–69), 1–10. The role of *Repulsion* in the director's evolution of new myths about communication.

———,"Dr Strangelove—Strange Loves and Stranger Deaths," *New Politics,* III (Spring, 1964), 94–99. The bomber and its crew seen as a monster on the loose.

Schöler, Franz, "Die Erben des Marquis de Sade," Horrorfilm Part I: Vampirismus in Literatur und Film, *Film,* V (August, 1967), 10–17. A scholarly and insightful critique of vampire films and their relation to literature.

———, "Die Erben des Marquis de Sade," Horrorfilm Part II: Zaroff, King Kong and Co., *Film,* V (September, 1967), 10–18. Continued in the style of the above, ending with an extensive filmography and bibliography of horror films and an interview with Barbara Steele.

———, "Die Erben des Marquis de Sade," Horrorfilm Part III: Frankenstein, Jekyll, and the Gothic Horror, *Film,* V (October, 1967), 12–19. Continued in the style of the above, with especially spectacular pictorial illustrations.

———, ed., "Horror-Bilderbuch und Materialien zu den literarischer Dorläufern des Horror-Films," *Film* V (November, 1967), 41–51. Pictures and excerpts from literary horror classics.

Tarratt, Margaret, "Monsters from the Id," *Films and Filming* (in two parts), December, 1970 and January, 1971. A Freudian analysis of symbolic impotence, frigidity, etc., in classic science-monster films.

* Thomas, John, "Freaks," *Film Quarterly,* XVII No. 3 (Spring, 1964), 59–61. A sensitive appreciation of *Freaks* as a form of antihorror. Published here as "Gobble, Gobble . . . One of Us!"

Torok, Jean-Paul, "H Pictures," *Positif,* No. 39 (May, 1961), 54–58; No. 40 (July, 1961), 41–49. A two-part history of the development of the horror genre in England.

* Troy, William, "Beauty and the Beast," *The Nation,* CXXXVI, No. 3533 (1933), 326. A review of the New York premiere of *King Kong,* focusing on the effects of size and perspective.

Weinberg, Herman and Gretchen, "*Vampyr*—An Interview with Baron de Gunzberg," *Film Culture,* No. 32 (Spring, 1964), 57–59. A detailed discussion of the working problems connected with the filming of Dreyer's classic.

Wood, Robin, "In Memoriam Michael Reeves," *Movie,* No. 17 (Winter, 1969–70), 2–6. A penetrating evaluation of the small but excellent core of horror films by the late director.

Wray, Fay, "How Fay Wray Met Kong, or the Scream That Shook the World," *The New York Times,* September 21, 1969, Sec. 4, p. 17. An amusing memoir on Miss Wray's contacts with her most famous leading man.

PERIODICALS

Bizarre (in French). Uneven, sometimes anecdotal. Often devoted to the life and career of a particular director or star.

Castle of Frankenstein. Hard to come by, but generally of a high quality.

Cinefantastique. A newcomer, containing technically detailed articles and extensive reviews of the fantasy-horror field.

Midi-Minuit Fantastique (in French). One of the most enduring and serious of the journals devoted to fantasy-horror.

Motion, No. 4 (February, 1963). This issue of the British journal is devoted to "Violence in the Cinema" and contains supplementary sections on horror films, including a section on the genre's pinup girl, Barbara Steele, "the only girl in films whose eyelids can snarl."

Index[1]

[1] Index covers pages 1–169 only.